THE ART OF ANCIENT PERU

I

HEINRICH UBBELOHDE-DOERING

THE ART
OF ANCIENT PERU

NEW YORK · FREDERICK A. PRAEGER
MCMLIV

Photographs: Museum für Völkerkunde, Berlin p. 33, 35 and 82, 96, 98 top. Brooklyn Museum p. 69, 90, 100, 105, 133, 148–153. Cleveland Museum of Art p. 108 bottom left. Göteborgs Museum p. 158, 159. Museum für Völkerkunde, Hamburg p. 56 right, 63–65. Museo Nacional de Arqueología, Lima p. 60, 61. American Museum of Natural History, New York p. 42, 228 top. The University Museum, Philadelphia p. 236 bottom. Linden-Museum, Stuttgart p. 207, 212, 230. Dr. Arndt, Frankfurt am Main p. 155. Amerika-Haus, Munich p. 32, 116, 191, 233. Ad. F. Bandelier p. 55 top. Dr. Bartels, Dortmund p. 35 top. v. Breymann, Lima p. 108 bottom right. Hans Holdt, Munich p. 40 top, 62 top left, 188. Archiv Seler p. 25. Julio C. Tello (Discovery of the Chavín Culture in Peru, American Antiquity, IX, 1) p. 236 top, 237, 238. Author p. 1–24, 26–31, 44, 45, 52, 54 bottom, 55 bottom, 59, 122–125, 166, 169, 172, 173, 180, 181, 198–200, 206, 216, 217, 239. Verlag Wasmuth p. 41, 51, 71, 75, 85, 99, 101, 134, 135, 137, 140 left, 163–165, 182, 202.

All other photographs: Museum für Völkerkunde, Munich (Phot. H. Stubenböck).

The photographs for the color plates: Brend'amour, Simhart & Co., Munich.

Books That Matter

Published in the United States of America in 1952 by Frederick A. Praeger, Inc., Publishers,
105 West 40th Street, New York 18, N. Y.
All Rights Reserved – Library of Congress Catalog Card Number: 52-7489
Published in Germany in 1952 by Verlag Ernst Wasmuth, Tübingen
Second edition 1954
Printed in Germany – Ensslin-Druck Reutlingen

PREFACE

Neither the publication of this book, nor the gathering of material would have been possible without the generous help and assistance of the Wenner-Gren Foundation, its Director, Dr. Paul Fejos, and the publishing house Ernst Wasmuth. The Wenner-Green Foundation enabled me to visit museums and collections in the United States and to study there many Ancient Peruvian masterpieces of highest quality. In spite of the great difficulties of post-war production, the publisher did everything in his power to bring out a book which can take its place among the best American and European art publications. I would like to express my gratitude to Dr. Fejos and to my friend, Guenther Wasmuth. I hope this book will do its share in spreading the fame and glory of Ancient Peruvian art.

Heinrich U.-Doering

Condor with wings stretched out
Stone carving from Chavín de Huantar. Copied by Humberto Hidalgo. After Bennett, Chavín Stone Carving.

INTRODUCTION

That Ancient Peruvian art is not identical with Inca art is a fact that has been stressed more than once in recent years. Only a small fraction of the many and diversified works of art which since the conquest of Peru in the 16th century were found within the orbit of the Inca Empire can be ascribed to the artists of that famous semi-divine dynasty. Thus, speaking of The Art of Ancient Peru we think also of the infinite wealth of Pre-Inca art as it grew in areas which only later came to be embodied in the Inca territory.

The art of the Incas, the last and latest in a sequence of stages covering at least two thousand years, was only one among several manifestations seen by the Spaniards when in 1532 they invaded the Peruvian countries. They also encountered other and different styles as they landed on the Northern coast, or proceeded to Cajamarca, or headed – under Hernando Pizarro, the conquistador's brother – for the Temple of Pachacamac, 'Creator of the World'. But, wherever the Spaniards came, Inca art – architecture, ceramics, textiles, and metalwork – had penetrated before them as though in a great flood, to which the spread of the Inca power and Inca culture during the 15th and 16th centuries A. D. may indeed be likened.

It was from Cuzco, capital of the Empire in the Southern Highlands, that those peculiar forms conventionally styled 'Inca' had radiated so powerfully: trapeziform gates, windows, and niches; the noble clay amphoras; large bowls of stone. Of none of them can be said with certainly whether they were Inca creations or whether they were produced in the Cuzco region perhaps long before the arrival of the Incas, in which case they should properly be spoken of as Cuzco art (Pls. 1–12, 18–21, 36, 37).

If in this book therefore – in contrast to others – materials are so arranged that the oldest hitherto known pieces appear at the end, we conform to the succession of the actual discoveries. We are accompanying, so to speak, the Spaniards of the early 16th century, and together with them observe the New World, which even in its late and often conventionalized images still shows an all-pervading faith. We accompany also the scholars of the 19th and 20th centuries who devoted themselves to the study and exploration of Old Peruvian history and art, and in the end arrive at the remotest past that science has thus far been able to penetrate – which may not however be defined with any confidence as a beginning.

An understanding of the fact that Ancient Peru cannot simply be equated with the Incas and *vice versa* was hardly gained before the second half of the 19th century, although from records taken down as early as the time of the Spanish viceroys we know of Indian statements about older kingdoms as well as about exploits, by no means purely mythical, from long before the Inca Empire. However, conclusions which could have been drawn from those accounts and a gradually widening knowledge – that conditions such as are found in descriptions of the 15th and 16th centuries cannot well have existed in cultures that flourished 1000 years earlier – actually were drawn only fairly recently or were not drawn at all.

Among the first to perceive the chronological depth of the ancient Peruvian cultures was Dr. E. W. Middendorf, who around 1880 travelled in the Cordillera and on the coast of Peru. He recognized and outlined one of the crucial problems of Peruvian archaeology, the Chavín problem, taken up so successfully later by Julio C. Tello. Around 1900 and during the first decades of the 20th century, a scheme of chronology, the sequence of cultures and their filiations, was drafted by Max Uhle. Many of the basic elements of his structure remain valid. His scholarly accomplishment must be rated the higher as he had to lay the very foundations; his excavations of the Pachacamac ruins and those near the pyramids of Moche were the first to be carried through systematically. As a result of his explorations at Moche, Uhle came to subdivide the mass of the archaeological finds from the North into several categories which he assigned to as many cultures, and to define their relative position as follows:

An early culture termed 'Proto-Chimú' (a term adopted widely among American archaeologists in the beginning but about to be replaced by the new term of 'Mochica'; pls. 168–227).

A later cultural stage under the influence of the Tiahuanaco culture (pls. 122–127), now called 'Coastal Tiahuanaco'.

A late culture termed 'Late Chimú', now called 'Chimú' (pls. 54–66).

Between 1900 and 1910, Uhle was active also in the South, in the Nazca Valleys, although according to Dr. Eduard Gaffron's statement it would appear that besides exploring and collecting there was little done in the way of actual excavation. Only from the more northerly Ica Valley do we have Uhle's reports on excavations, but they are not very detailed and reveal little of his methods of digging. However, attempting to collocate the archaeological remains of the South also, Uhle separated an early 'Proto-Nazca Culture', now simply 'Nazca' (pls. 134–144) – from a late 'Ica Culture', called after the main sites, in the Valley of the Rio Grande de Ica (pls. 84–87) – placing a 'Coastal Tiahuanaco Culture' – as in the North – between them (pls. 93–116). The two early cultures in the North and the South, Mochica and Nazca, were placed in the first five centuries by Uhle, who was inclined to consider Nazca slightly the earlier of the two.

In the second decade of the 20th century, the Peruvian archaeologist Julio C. Tello rose to eminence. In this extraordinarily able man, a passionate love of his country's ancient past was combined with a strong intuitive faculty that guided him to perceive ever new problems, a working power that was indefatigable, and an unparalleled knowledge of most of the sites along the coast and in the mountains of both the Western and Eastern Cordillera. One had the impression that day and night he pondered over the great problems which confronted him and searched for the solutions which he sometimes had sensed beforehand. Thus he had intuitively recognized and understood the fundamental importance of the entire Chavín problem. His discovery of the Necropolis of Paracas, with its embroidered 'mantos' (pls. 148–152, 154) ranks among the most important of recent times, as does his discovery of the Temple Fronts in the Casma and Nepeña Valleys, which belong to the early stage (pls. 237, 238). Setting before himself ever new aims and tasks, Tello, wherever he carried his spade, time and again opened new sources of archaeological knowledge. Occasional disagreement with one or the other of his theses which may have been tainted by his ardent pride in the country's ancient grandeur does not impair his scientific position. Peruvian archaeology, after Tello's deplorably early death in 1947, is no longer the same as that which he found when he started.

Also in the twenties began the work of A. L. Kroeber on the Northern and the Southern Coasts. Directing his eyes more and more toward the totality of the archaeological phenomena, examining, sifting, comparing them, he put forth new problems with a carefully balanced and considered judgment. He went over the collections of Max Uhle in Berkeley and edited them in cooperation with Duncan Strong and Lila O'Neale.

With Kroeber are at work a galaxy of successful younger archaeologists: Wendell C. Bennet, Junius Bird, Donald Collier, James Ford, Alfred Kidder II, John H. Rowe, William Duncan Strong, Richard Schaedel and Gordon Willey. Their efforts are devoted to stratigraphy, in the first place; to the execution of stratified diggings in refuse heaps; to vertical cuts showing objects, notably ceramics, in their safe relative positions, such as are likely to lead – and have led – to a relative chronology. In our section on Chronology below, their conclusions and theses will be discussed.

In Peru itself, too, a school has formed, whose members tend to specialize in the study of particular fields or cultures. Rebeca Carrión Cachot, who cooperated with Tello, has chosen the Chavín culture in its various aspects as her favoured subject; Luis E. Valcárcel's interest is chiefly devoted to the culture of the Incas and their centre, Cuzco. With them are Muelle, Mejía, and the unforgettable Yakov Ieff, who died young. A place apart is held by Rafael Larco Hoyle, collector and connoisseur of note, whose archaeological merits are connected chiefly with the elucidation of the early periods of Northern Peru. The 'Museo Victor Larco Herrera' as it stands today in the Chiclín Hacienda (Chicama Valley), with its peerless, precious collections of works of art of the Mochica culture and other early cultures of the North, goes to his credit.

The endeavours of the present writer and of his collaborator, H. D. Disselhoff, were mainly directed toward the uncovering of untouched tombs, the contents as well as the structure of which were considered as units. Stratigraphical data – always a rarity in grave-fields – were of course taken into account as they occurred. Both goals are of course equally important: To work out a chronology based on "facts" established through the examination of stratified layers and to draw a comprehensive and clearly defined picture of the material and spiritual culture of the ancient Peruvian empires and peoples and their mutual chronological relations through the comparative investigations of tomb-units.

Thus far we have been told nothing about art, the reader may say. True, the work of all those just mentioned and their scholarly contributions are concerned with archaeology. Their methods are archaeological methods. Much of what they did and could achieve may seem dry and unexciting. However, it would be quite wrong to think of the result of their efforts as amounting finally to such humble objects as sherds of clay, shreds of cloth and the like, and to a lifeless chronology. At the end of their work in dust and dirt there will reappear – as old paintings re-emerge from dust and turbid varnish – the life and the fate of the 'Flower Folk' (as Stucken once called the Mexicans of the past), a mythical folk, men of fairy-tales – not rarely terrible fairy-tales – whose world was different from ours: without iron but with gold; without wheels and chariots and draught-animals but with sedan-chairs; a world which may have been like that of the Pharaohs or the rulers of Uruk and Larsa. Had the Sumerians of the 3rd millenium B.C. disembarked in front of the Peruvian brick pyramids, they might have understood that world and that world would have understood them. The Spaniards entered these countries as Aladdin with the magic lamp entered the gardens glittering with precious stones: they understood neither the material side nor the spiritual side, and the latter in particular was sealed to them. It is archaeology which unlocks, one by one, the gates into that world of terror and beauty – terror in *our* conception, beauty in *our* conception – where grew the works that appear in the following plates. It is archaeology which presents to us these works of art and tries to make them speak to us.

Thus, the archaeologist is the discoverer of Ancient Peruvian art. All those named and many others beside them have done work for the sake of art, searching and finding it in ever darker depths of the past. Comparative study of the objects in the collections can be grossly misleading. The portrait-heads of the Mochica culture, for instance, have been taken as unquestionably late works created in Inca times (pls. 198 to 225), while in fact they sprang from a culture which not only had no contact with that of the Incas, but had vanished long before the Inca Empire had come into existence. It was Uhle's excavations at the foot of the Pyramid of the Moon near Moche that led to recognition of this. Of course, northern art did not begin with these sculptures. In fact, there were much older works of art there, those of Chavín, as we now know (pls. 235–239); but it seems impossible to trace back to those daemonic images of Chavín the very realistically rendered faces of Mochica art. Were it not for archaeological research, we should remain ignorant of the fact that the Mochica portraits followed those from Chavín but preceded the art of the Inca Empire. More dates such as these will have to be provided by the archaeologists before a history of the art of Ancient Peru can be written.

Archaeological research within the boundaries of the Inca Empire has led to the recognition of three different art-styles, each of which had spread so widely as to take on a Pan-Peruvian character: the Inca style or Cuzco style, about 12th to 16th centuries A. D. (pls. 1–21, 32–51); the Tiahuanaco style – called Coastal Tiahuanaco as it appears along the Coast – about 6th to 10th centuries A. D. (pls. 93–127); and the Chavín style – Coastal Chavín, at the Coast, about 2nd to 4th centuries A. D.

The cultures typified by works of art of any of these styles must have extended over vast areas of Western South America, as examples of them are found scattered over many regions of the later Inca Empire. Perhaps it is more appropriate, at least in the case of the two earlier styles, Tiahuanaco and Chavín, to speak not of cultures or kingdoms which had radiated so powerfully, but of far-reaching mental affinities whence similar art forms grew. Of the Inca style we know that it wandered with the widening frontiers of the realm, reaching finally the Equator in the North and Chile in the South, the tropical forests in the East and the sea in the West, and making its appearance wherever the Incas sent their armies, their officials, and their colonists.

It was formerly assumed that the carriers of the Tiahuanaco style were a nation of megalithic builders whose sway was felt still farther than that of the Incas. However, as nothing of an empire of such grandeur is actually known, we would do better to refer to the explanation pointed out above, viz., that the monuments of this style bear witness to intellectual affinities met with far and wide. Still, there ought to have been some powerful centre where this style was formed and from whence it spread. That the eponymic ruins of Tiahuanaco near the Lake of Titicaca at 13 000 feet above sea-level must not be taken as that centre, but rather as the place of the most mature manifestation of this style, can hardly be questioned.

The Chavín style poses the same questions. Again it seems unlikely that we should have to deal with a homogeneous culture or nation; instead, a world of images common to different groups and varying with them may have to be taken as the underlying unity. Even more than in the case of the Tiahuanaco stage which is younger by centuries, do we depend on the spade of the archaeologist for a final answer. While some dim light occasionally falls on the world of Tiahuanaco, darkness reigns over the centuries of the Chavín culture and the migrations and modifications of its great religious symbols. We know of these symbols, reflected in the works of art, but may not presume to have deciphered them.

In their architecture, all the peoples building in either of the two earlier styles, Tiahuanaco and Chavín, apparently preferred construction in stone. Conceivably these peoples were mountain folk, although many of their tombs and sanctuaries can be found on the coast. The problem arising here may conveniently be formulated in this question: Were the mountains the land of the living, and the coast the land of the dead for the peoples whose characteristic styles had been the Tiahuanaco, the Chavín – and perhaps get others, of local origin?

Although in the period of the later styles, including the Inca style, there existed at the coast a flourishing culture of oases with artificial irrigation and large cities such as Chanchán in the country of the Chimú, it appears questionable whether anything comparable had been there during the preceding centuries. The dwelling places – towns and villages – in the coastal valleys are all more recent, dating as they do from the 11th to 16th centuries A. D., whereas the constructions of the preceding millenium are sanctuaries or places of worship large and small, with the priests' and servants' houses clustered around them. Had lay settlements been established at the coast in the times of the middle and early cultures of the 1st millenium A. D., then we should be able to locate the ruins, which in this rainless desert-region ought to have survived. I know of none that could with certainty be ascribed to the Tiahuanaco culture, much less to older ones, whereas small sanctuaries and tombs even from the oldest times are encountered everywhere along the coast.

It might be argued that houses of the early periods were constructed of perishable materials such as wooden posts, wicker-work and mud, houses which could have vanished without leaving traces. The argument, however, implies that the technique of construction jumped from the mud-house stage to a stage of solid walls of bricks or pounded earth such as we find them in the later settlements – notwithstanding the fact that mud-houses did exist along with the more solidly built ones. Moreover, the early periods knew wall-constructions of conical bricks, for instance in the Nazca Valleys, in buildings which, few in number, may have served the purposes of the cult.

For these reasons I think that during the millenium preceding the later cultures, the coastal desert of Peru was possibly something like a land of the dead and of the gods; in the quiet loneliness of the desert, the mountain folk buried their dead and erected pyramids and terraces for those of their gods who were concerned with the sea and somehow – as the location of these sanctuaries amidst graveyards would suggest – also with the dead. That these dead appeared, after their transfiguration, in the community of the gods or semi-divine beings is evident from many of the ancient images.

The sight of the mountains, viewed perhaps from the Nazca Valleys on a hot day in the southerly summer, aptly illustrates a situation that hardly differs from what it must have been then: the mountains under summer rains, dazzling in emerald-green, like the Land of Promise; the desert below, dry and glowing, housing the tombs, Land of the Dead.

A theory such as is submitted above does not entirely preclude the possible existence of some local cultural centres at the coast during the 1st millenium A. D. They are probably responsible for the matchless polychromy of the Nazca painted pottery (pls. 134–144) or for the culture that created the magnificently embroidered fabrics discovered by Tello in the necropolis of Paracas (pls. 147–159). It is an open question, on the other hand, whether the cultures reflected in those finds from Nazca and Paracas Necropolis were located in the areas of the respective grave-fields or whether they should not be looked for in the mountains, more exactly in the western ranges close to the coast, the 'Ceja de la Costa' ('Brow of the Coast'), as they are called. The iconography of the Paracas 'mantos' proves conspicuously akin to that of works in Tiahuanaco style. This affinity raises the question whether the origin of these fabrics should not be looked for in a still hypothetical Early Tiahuanaco in the mountains. In both Nazca and Paracas cultures – older Paracas Cavernas as well as the later Paracas Necropolis – radiations from the mountains would appear to have united with some from a different, still enigmatic focus in the North, South, or overseas.

Even if remains of small settlements could be shown to be connected with sanctuaries or with ceramics of the Chavín or Mochica cultures, they yet would hardly represent the habitations left by either of these cultures. Coastal Chavín cannot possibly have been generated by a few villagers and hut-dwellers. Nor can the meagre architectural remains found in the coastal desert of the Bay of Paracas be taken as the cradle and actual home of the art of Paracas. For it is out of the question that the skilled people who produced the marvellous embroideries discovered by the hundreds in that necropolis should have lived in the tiny fishermen-huts or subterranean dwellings found by Tello. The art of Paracas certainly presupposed large communities thriving on higher agriculture, with a differentiated social hierarchy, and the possession of a replete, codified, as it were, repertory of religious images. No community of this kind, however, has ever existed at Paracas. Their habitat has yet to be found.

The problem posed here is corroborated to some extent in a few further observations. In one of the valleys of the Northern Coast, the Chicama Valley, the finest ceramics of typical Mochica style (that is, about 5th to 9th centuries A.D.) were encountered by us in a small pyramid erected on top of a bastion-like steep spur commanding the wide space of the valley. The scenery is entirely foreign to the Coast. Here, these ceramics were associated with sharp-cornered dressed stones. The foundation of the pyramid and a portion of its interior structure consisted exclusively of this sort of ashlar, as did the walls and ceilings of the tombs, the contents of which were of unadulterated Mochica style throughout. Not one brick was found.

The great importance of the *Ceja de la Costa*, the Cordillera close to the coast, has been stressed also by Kroeber. Possibly the Mochica culture had grown in those mountains; one or several peoples of those mountains may have produced the abundant painted and modelled Mochica ceramics, especially for the cult of the dead; perhaps along with a craft in clay or stone not hitherto rediscovered, or an industry whose connection with what we call Mochica has remained in the dark thus far.

A concentration and preponderance of worship and ritual along the coast seems to be indicated also by the magnitude of the religious architecture in the ruins of Pacatnamú at the Northern Coast with an array of more than 60 pyramids and stepped terraces of various sizes. When excavating there in 1937/38, I had but one explanation for the phenomenon of these many structurally uniform complexes, namely, that a multitude of communities or tribes from the mountain valleys near and far had buried their dead here, close to the shore, and that they used funerary gifts of the same style or similar styles. This style, the Mochica style, embracing different ethnical groups, was mixed here with forms belonging to Coastal Chavín and 'Gallinazo' (or 'Negative') styles.

Sacrifices of llamas occurring in many early tombs at the coast again point to the mountains as their likely origin. Conceivably, these llamas, animals of the mountains which as beasts of burden even today descend only to return quickly, came down to the coast with funeral processions. In the shaft-graves and other coeval tombs at Pacatnamú, we uncovered many skeletal remains of llamas; apparently they had some ritual significance, as their scapulas were almost invariably fastened to the lids of the coffins. In the large shaft-graves on the Morro of Cahuachi in the Rio Grande de Nazca Valley, I met llama sacrificial interments everywhere, particularly at the bottom of the upper 'pozo', close to the edges of the lower 'pozo' or true burial chamber.

People who in their funerary ritual used the llama – an animal essential to their daily life – so widely and as a matter of course, must have lived in the mountains. Trade relations cannot explain the trips. These would have presupposed a developed cultural set-up at the coast in possession of manifold items of exchange. But why should those mountain people have brought their dead down to the hot coast that was not their homeland? The conclusion seems unavoidable that they guided the dead to the land where in those people's belief the transfiguration of the dead into new forms of existence took place.

Only later and gradually did mountain folk begin to enter the Land of the Dead and the Gods to cultivate the ground between temples and sepulchres. Seafaring people, too, may have landed and erected sanctuaries such as that near Lambayeque in the North, where Naymlap, the strange king, appeared with his *cortège* on balsa floats and founded a dynasty. To the present day, nobody can safely say from whence he came. However, the foreigners from the sea were few in number when compared to the multitude of the aborigines in the mountains, and they came only late, probably after 1000 A.D. Thus, the late cultures at the coast came into being by a blending of two constituents, that from the mountains and that from the coast or the sea. Quantitatively speaking, the first and older of the two is by far the more powerful one. Qualitatively, the two component cultures are difficult to compare or assess. At any rate, without the element having come by way of the sea, the coastal culture of the last centuries before the discovery of Peru would look different from what it actually became.

The chief contributions had come from the mountains. All Pan-styles, and perhaps several others, had been styles of the mountains. It was with mountain folk that stone building reached the coast. Stone was their proper medium of self-expression. From the westernmost Cordillera, rising over the torrid, feverish valleys that open toward the coastal desert, mountain folk descended to the Land of the Dead even before 1000 A. D. However, these wandering tribes, forerunners of those who made themselves masters of the lowlands, still kept to the heights, where we find the remains of their dwelling-places. The valleys still were the domain of the dead, but their tabu must have begun to fade by then.

Along the shore, at the other edge of the desert-like coastal plains, poor fishermen may have lived since the earliest times. Their cultural contribution was hardly an essential one. They may, however, have been responsible for a ceramic-less culture such as that discovered by Bird at the Northern Coast. Unquestionably, this primitive culture persisted from the oldest times down to the decline of the Inca Empire.

From the mountains came most of the ancient cultures: Chavín, and a hypothetical Pre-Chavín; Gallinazo; Tiahuanaco; Paracas Cavernas; Epigonal (Morro); Chanca; and others still. As to Nazca, Paracas Necropolis, and Mochica, there is increasing evidence that their origins were also in the mountains. The great rôle attributed by Tello to the Andinium as the focus of the Ancient Peruvian cultures inclusive of those at the coast seems convincing in many regards.

One more word has to be said in connection with the whole problem. The occurrence of art objects at a certain place does not necessarily presuppose that their makers – as sometimes it is taken for granted – were settled there. Likewise, the occurrence of refuse heaps does not necessarily imply that at these places there were communities leading a settled life. Mighty heaps of refuse containing all sorts of animal and vegetable remains, as well as articles of every-day life, as carried by the funeral caravans or used by priests and temple-servants, can well have developed during a span of thousand or more years. Ritual feasting on top of the mud-platforms over the grave-pits – a habit known to us also from Sumer (Anton Moortgat, Geschichte Vorderasiens bis zum Hellenismus, Munich, 1950, p. 250) obviously was practised at Pacatnamú; when excavating there in 1938, we found scores of llama bones, traces of food, ashes, pottery, textiles, basketry. Refuse heaps must have piled up also near the camps of the many pilgrims and worshippers. However, whether left by settlers or pilgrims, the chronological value of the layers in these heaps remains the same.

The chronology of Ancient Peru is based on a fairly reliable tradition only for the late pre-Spanish times of the Inca Empire. Somewhat farther back, in the 14th and 13th centuries A. D. and still in Inca times, dusk begins, and as soon as we try to penetrate into the more remote past before 1000 A. D., we are in a dark unlit by any written or oral tradition. Ancient Peru, magnificent though its material and spiritual creations are, has remained without a script, and for no less than three quarters of its history there is not a single fact reported upon which to base a chronology. The light of some myths, it is true, does shine dimly from Peru's far past, but there is nothing in them to be used in a well-founded chronological system. Here, only the archaeologist or prehistorian can help us further.

An ingenious intuition may be able to reveal some of the major processes of the past, recognize problems, indicate the direction for future research. A chronological diagram, however, requires facts that have to be established by a minute archaeological investigation. It would cover and classify thousands of chronologically floating objects in public and private collections, determine their relative positions within the ancient cultures and art styles, and eventually arrive at their absolute chronology. This kind of diagram will not be found in the book. It could create the impression of more knowledge and more established facts than would be warranted by the results of our research. A diagram based solely on established facts would appear too meagre to the layman and for the expert would have to be confirmed through detailed scientific data. Chronological diagrams for geographically limited regions, which are based on methodical excavations, such as those in the Virú Valley, can be considered the best premises for a general diagram, which covers the entire chronology of Ancient Peru.

The ideal result of an excavation aiming at chronological evidence is a clear sequence of layers. Sequences of this sort are only rarely found in grave-fields, whereas they are commonly found in refuse heaps as encountered in many archaeological sites from the earliest periods onward. During recent years, American archaeologists have with good results carried out systematic diggings of stratified refuse heaps at the Northern and Central Peruvian Coasts (Chicama and Virú Valley in the North; Pachacamac and Lurín Valley at the Central Coast).

Three Pan-Peruvian styles at certain epochs are almost ubiquitous: the Inca style of the 15th and early 16th centuries; the Tiahuanaco style, about 500 years or more earlier; and the Chavín style, of which we can say hardly more than that it was in vogue on the whole before 500 A. D.

The intervals between the Pan-styles are filled with styles which, as far as our knowledge goes, appear to have been developed in particular regions: the Mochica style in the North (pls. 168–227); the Nazca style (pls. 134–144) and the two Paracas styles (Paracas Necropolis and Paracas Cavernas) (pls. 145–159 and 160, 161, 239) in the South. Some of these regional styles should probably be placed on the same level or with an overlapping at both the beginning and the end. Possibly some of these styles will, as a consequence of new excavation results, have to be interchanged, as might be the case with Nazca and Paracas Necropolis. In case one or another regional style should show a tendency toward widening into a Pan-style, further revisions of the diagram would become necessary. The Mochica style, for instance, reappears in a slightly altered form in fabrics of the Nazca region (Colour Plate III), the age of which cannot accurately be made out thus far.

However that may be, on the whole it seems that the picture is taking shape, and for several areas – e. g., the Virú Valley at the Northern Coast – the sequence of most of the cultures and styles has been definitely established through dependable stratigraphic excavations. Unfortunately, the safest results obtained in a narrowly limited area cannot simply be transferred to another, even adjacent, area or be generalized. For every valley, rather even every section of it, the sequence of the cultures and styles will have to be worked out individually. Then only will it be possible for the sequences of wider areas and, ultimately, of the entire Andean West of South America to be determined on broader lines.

All of the Pan-styles must have originated somewhere. Somewhere the first crystallization of a style must have taken place to be able to call forth – as the style-engendering stratum expanded – ever new crystallizations until a Pan-style came into being.

The home of the Inca style (or Cuzco style) was most likely in the area of the ancient capital of the Inca Empire, Cuzco. The cradle of the Tiahuanaco style, on the other hand, which seemingly had spread farther even than the Inca style, has not been traced so far. It would appear that the region of Ayacucho in the Southern Highlands is being given increasing attention as a relevant critical zone, and the ruin-city of Huari in just that area has risen like a new star in the archaeological sky of Peru. The uniqueness and incomparable grandeur of the famous patronymic ruins of Tiahuanaco would not be affected by the assumption of the Tiahuanaco style having originated elsewhere. The Tiahuanaco monuments remain among the greatest achievements of the arts of Ancient America.

Nor can anything be safely said regarding the centre of origin of the Chavín style, which in essential features is akin to the Tiahuanaco style but contains a component of passionate ferocity absent in the latter. Again it seems that the patronymic ruins of Chavín de Huantar on the Eastern Cordillera Blanca do not represent the actual centre, although the large and copiously ornamented stone images testify to the importance of that place. Similar to the Tiahuanaco style, that of Chavín exhibits – within the orbit of the general style – much variation in the details. The underlying spiritual concepts no doubt came to be

14

embodied in the art of widely different human groups and the resulting stylistic variations sometimes appear hardly related to each other.

There are facts which suggest that the most ancient hearth of the Chavín style might one day be found in the hills of the *Ceja de la Costa*, (Brow of the Coast), and in the western ranges of the Cordillera. Tello was inclined to look to the East for the sources of the great currents of culture as well as the basic elements of the main styles. It is close to the Amazonas forest region but still in the mountain valleys of the Cordillera, as he pointed out to me one day, that the oldest strata of the Chavín culture are found close to the surface, with hardly any overlying admixtures, while the same Chavín remains are buried lowermost under numerous layers of different cultures in the coastal plains of the West; these facts would seem to indicate that there were no cultural movements from West to East and no chance for later cultures to overlay the earliest ones in the East.

Various regional styles, chronologically still somewhat unsettled, are found between these Pan-styles. In terms of the absolute chronology, they are drifting through the centuries, sometimes being brought closer to the present, sometimes pushed back into the past, as new finds demand a change of opinions. Similarly, there are shifts in the relative chronology of these styles whenever some successful stratified excavation permits to establish a definite sequence of driving in, as it were, a solid hook. However, it then happens sometimes that on this one hook are suspended all of the known occurrences of one style or one culture, all of them being taken as belonging to the same chronological level. This is the case with the Mochica style. In the Virú Valley, Duncan Strong uncovered a clear, stratified sequence of the Northern styles following the Chavín style: Salinar – Gallinazo (Negative style) – Mochica. Thus, in the Virú Valley, the Mochica style is later than the Gallinazo style. Our own excavations in the Jequetepeque Valley (north of Trujillo), on the other hand, yielded pottery of Gallinazo style side by side with pottery of Mochica style and even a Chavinoid style, unless this latter has to be defined as a variant of the Coastal Chavín style, as Tello assuredly would have done (pl. 234). In a small pyramid of the Chicama Valley (Licapa IV), excavated by myself in 1938, negative-paint sherds of Gallinazo style came to light in a Post-Mochica section of the structure.

Thus, in three valleys of the same region we have to deal with three different chronological sequences: Gallinazo before Mochica; Gallinazo coeval with Mochica; and Gallinazo after Mochica. The shaft-tombs of Pacatnamú show that at this site Chavín, Gallinazo, and Mochica were all contemporary. Allowance must therefore be made for some style or other to have continued, in particular sites, through many centuries; styles which elsewhere would follow one after the other.

In the South, the chronological relationship between Paracas Necropolis (pls. 145–159) and Nazca styles (pls. 134–144) is a problem that remains to be solved: are the embroidered fabrics discovered by Tello in the Necropolis of Paracas older than the colourful vessels of the Nazca culture or *vice versa?* What were, generally, the relations between Nazca and Paracas? It can hardly be doubted that the pottery from Paracas Cavernas with the contours of the painting incised (pls. 160, 161, 239) is older than the polychrome Nazca wares. From the Necropolis of Paracas, however, have come no vessels with similarly outlined images, either chavinesque or tiahuanacoid. Thus, in regard to their mutual relationship, the Nazca and Paracas Necropolis styles still remain floating islands.

Similarly wavering is the position of the Epigonal, or, as I have proposed to call it, Morro style in relation to the Tiahuanaco style. That the Epigonal or Morro style did not come after the Tiahuanaco style is doubtless a safe supposition, and it seems reasonable to assume that it preceded the latter. In the Nazca Valleys, the Morro style appears not to have been fully coeval with the strange cubical style we meet there. Going farther back, we find that the Morro style distinctly still overlaps with the Nazca style. It becomes apparent that the Morro style extends back as far as the Nazca style and lasts into the phase of Coastal Tiahuanaco. This fact may become important for the solution of one of the cardinal questions of Peruvian archaeology: the question of the origin and the centre of the Tiahuanaco style.

Another cardinal problem is that of the origins and the focus of the Chavín style. And a third problem is connected with both Tiahuanaco and Chavín: how far are these two grand styles related to each other? A problem much harder to answer than would first appear.

The style of Pucara (region of Lake Titicaca; pl. 128), too, has not been securely anchored as yet in either relative or absolute chronology. Some have equated it with the Tiahuanaco and Mochica styles, while others believe it to have preceded those styles and accordingly would place it in the lower zone of the regional styles between the two older Pan-styles. Its similarity to the Tiahuanaco style – in this latter's symbolism – springs to the eyes. However, reflexes of the Chavín style seem also to be present in the Pucara style.

These unavoidable chronological discussions do not, of course, exhaust the subject. They are only to show the main intricacies of that chronology, to give the reader an idea of the difficulties encountered in advancing into Peru's scriptless past, and to bring to his attention the extent to which known facts are still outnumbered by hypotheses.

Besides stratified excavations and other archaeological methods, the tree ring chronology (dendro-chronology) and the radiocarbon method will certainly prove helpful in defining the relative and absolute ages of the antiquities. The tree ring chronology is based on the determination of the age of wooden beams and rafters in buildings or tombs – and consequently the age of those structures in themselves – through counting the number of the annual rings and comparing these rings with those of living old trees of the same area, a procedure which on account of the specific character of the individual rings and sequences of rings leads to a concordance at some definite point.

The radiocarbon-dating method is based on the discovery of nuclear-physical processes. These consist in that nuclei of atmospheric carbon C-14 contained in organic remains, disintegrate in the course of several thousand years by discharging electrons. The time in which half of the C-14 nuclei of an organic substance has disintegrated is 5568 ± 30 years. This radiocarbon-dating method developed by W. F. Libby and I. R. Arnold makes it possible to count the number of C-14 nuclei at any time present in organic matter, thus determining its approximate age within a margin of ca. $200-300$ years.

This method was used with great success in the case of archaeological finds from Egypt and Mexico and has led to corrections of many dates previously upheld. For Ancient Peru, too, both methods are promising.

The sequence of styles as discussed above by no means implies that those styles simply grew out of the preceding ones. This holds good for the Tiahuanaco style which follows upon the Mochica style, as well as for the Chimú and Ica styles which come after the Tiahuanaco style; and the same is true of the Salinar style which succeeds the Chavín style. It is impossible to think of the somewhat clumsy and primitive style of Salinar as derived from a style in which were created masterpieces such as the stone reliefs and the well-nigh grandiose ceramics of Chavín. These two styles have hardly anything in common. The Ica style of the Southern Coastal area proves slightly tinged by the Tiahuanaco style that preceded it, but even so is quite *sui generis* and strangely isolated all along the coast; it almost looks as though the Ica style had resulted from a tribal relocation such as for political considerations were carried out under the Incas, a relocation which in this case may have started from the Eastern slopes of the Cordillera. For the ornaments of the Ica ceramics give the impression of being derivatives of basket patterns (pl. 84), and the everted rims likewise are reminiscent of basket rims. However, the possibility of a migration of one or several tribes from the Montana, the tropical mountain forests of the East, across the Andes *prior* to the intrusion of the Incas has to be considered. Eduard Seler (*Gesammelte Abhandlungen*, Vol. IV, p. 244) has already pointed out that among the images of the Nazca paintings there occur parrots of a kind known only from the eastern side of the Andes. This fact would bespeak an influence in a period long before the Incas descended down to the Southern Coast, and with it we are reminded once more of Tello's abovementioned thesis of the Andean cultures having their roots quite generally in the East.

16

Summing up, we may say that the ancient cultures of Peru and the various regional and Pan-styles they produced seem to have covered a period of nearly 2000 years, a period that ended in the catastrophe of Cajamarca, 1532. Beyond that period, which is subdivided in accordance with the styles of the main ceramics, a pre-ceramic older past has been unveiled through Junius Bird's excavations, which yielded simple implements and basket-work but no pottery. And, earlier still, long before that pre-ceramic age, primitive Stone Age hunters were roaming the hills, greener than nowadays, close to the Northern Coast. Possibly those hunters still encountered some now extinct mammals such as, for instance, a giant water-hog, as our investigations of artifacts and Pleistocene fossil remains in the Pampa of Mocan ('Cupisnique') in 1937/38 make us believe.

What the Ancient Peruvian art styles are like is best seen in the reproductions of the objects themselves. If you look at them, beginning with the Inca period, you will find, in the first place, plain, noble, often truly restrained works of art (such as the big amphorae, pl. 36), an art which at the same time, particularly in architecture and in the stone serpent-bowls (pl. 35), does not lack a quiet force. Delicacy, too, is found in vase paintings and the works of the goldsmiths. You may feel reminded of Chinese art of the Han Dynasty, which shows rococo-like lacquer-work side by side with grand and powerful monuments.

When on our pilgrimage through the ages we have passed the Inca zone, we shall come, in the North, to the big cities of the Chimús where we meet with a somewhat conventionalized art of sculptured and relieved pottery which but rarely charms the onlooker immediately (pls. 57, 58); at the Central Coast we encounter the very peculiar and unmistakably late pottery of Chancay (pls. 73, 74) with greyish yellow or greyish white body and often covered by a chocolate-coloured slip. Finally, in the South we see the pots and bowls of the Ica style, which appear as if caned in basket-work (pl. 84). The monument-like round towers of the Chullpa culture, which rise into the thin air of the Titicaca Highland, may have been erected by then (pls. 52, 53).

Next we arrive in a zone of an all-dominating style, the Tiahuanaco style in its two distinct versions: the one, a world of images in cubic, rectangular forms, condensed symbols, so to speak (pls. 94, 95, 97–103); the other, a realistic art that skips unimportant detail as well as outspokenly individual traits and aims at a monumental grandeur (pls. 109–119). Two worlds, as different as those of the dead and the living. Yet, something of the awesome air of the life beyond, that of the spirit world in the symbolic style, seems to pervade also the world of man, much as an earthly warmth prevails in not a few of the works of the realistic style.

Having traversed this strangest of the realms of ancient Peruvian art, we again face a mosaic of manifold cultures and styles. In the North, the *crème de la crème* of Peruvian art: the Mochica pottery, exquisitely painted in India red on yellowish white, sometimes with a broad brush, sometimes with a pointed one and in a miniature-like fineness; or moulded in plastic shapes depicting a multitude of subjects, among which a unique group stands out: a gallery of portraits which might well be termed a Westminster Abbey of Old Peru, if only we knew the names and dates of the portrayed or were able to report of their deeds (pls. 203 to 225). The great diversity of the thoroughly individually treated faces and the fact of their close similarities to the physiognomies of modern Indians living in the Southern Highlands (cp. H. Ubbelohde-Doering, Auf den Königstraßen der Inca, pls. 112–119, 130–137, 148–153) make it likely that those portraits are representative of the whole of ancient Peru rather than of a particular tribe only.

Parallel and anterior to Mochica art, we see works of a lesser quality and a more primitive kind: those of Gallinazo and Salinar styles. They are hardly qualified to be taken as forerunners of the Mochica style. In the South we have a complex which in spite of various affinities remains rather baffling. This complex centres around the Nazca pottery, a ware painted in bright colours, without anything in Ancient America to match it, and the cruder wares of the Epigonal or Morro culture, associated in turn with a phenomenal textile art (pls. 130–133) for which the Nazca culture was given undeserved credit. Holding an unparalleled level of refinement, textile art reaches a culminating point in the embroidered *mantos* of Paracas, those hitherto undeciphered books of a people who lived in their beliefs as in dreams (pls. 148–152, 154–159).

And then dawns before our eyes what to our present knowledge appears to be the last and oldest zone, that of the Chavín style, offshoots of which are likely to have appeared here and there in the regional field we just traversed. The Chavín style manifested itself in works of art that vibrate with an almost fierce religious faith. Any stroke of the modelling-tool in the clay is done with so passionate a force that, even when found as the only trace in a fragment, it would in itself contain the whole style, its *verve*, all its terrors and all its grandeur. If there is any style to show the 'tremendum' in the highest degree, it is the style of Chavín. Close to it, that of Tiahuanaco.

Condor with Jaguar-fangs
Fragment of a stone carving from Chavín de Huantar. Copied by Humberto Hidalgo.
After Bennett, Charvín Stone Carving

NOTES ON THE COLOUR PLATES

I. Feather Cloak. The quill of each feather has been broken and fastened to two cotton threads running traverse on the cotton ground-warp. Wherever the feathers coincide with the outlines of the picture, their beard has been carefully cut off. The colours of the feathers are extremely brilliant and often well-nigh radiant. The two crowned figures of deities carry in their lifted hands a sceptre ending in an animal head. From their sides, green, angular volutes come forth. The inner side of the cloak is trimmed with larger, kingfisher blue, opalescent feathers. Length 95 cm., width 110 cm. Estaquería, Valley of Rio Grande de Nazca. Coastal Tiahuanaco Culture (Tiahuanaco Costeño), ca. 700 to 900 A. D. Museum für Völkerkunde, Munich.

II. Part of a cloak in Gobelin technique, with stylised llamas chequer-wise arranged (each two connected at their corners); ceremonial colours alternating.
Width of portion shown: 40 cm. Nazca Region, S. Peru. Inca Culture, 13th to 16th centuries A.D. Museum für Völkerkunde, Munich.

III. Tapestry, with slits partly sewed up with individual threads (clearly visible at top in the staff-like part of the warrior's wing). The upper and lower warrior have wings and bird tails. All three figures carry clubs in their hands, the lower even six; in addition, the two lower ones are on either side surrounded by clubs (for which the upper lacks space) thus demonstrating the character of the figures just as added hieroglyphs would do. From their mouth emerges a band indicating speaking or singing, as so far almost exclusively known from vase paintings and textiles of the Coastal Tiahuanaco and 'Epigonal' or Morro culture. In their general appearance as well as in their crescent-shaped, helmet-like head-dress, and clubs, these figures wholly resemble those painted on vases of the Mochica culture (N. Peru, between 400 and 600 A. D.). It seems to me indisputable that here a Mochica influence on the Nazca valleys – from which region of S. Peru this rare example comes – is recognizable. Though it is difficult to date this piece definitely, it could well be attributed to the 'Epigonal' or 'Morro culture' in part seemingly still coeval with the Nazca culture between ca. 500 and 800 A. D. From Huayurí Valley or Valley of the Rio Grande de Nazca, S. Peru. Museum für Völkerkunde, Munich.

IV. Embroidery on a fragment of a large blanket with chequer pattern, from Paracas (Necropolis): A sea god, a counterpart of Poseidon, and, beside him, a huge leaping fish. The head of the god is turned upward thus giving the impression that his face is upside down (turning the book that way his head becomes clearly recognizable, with a red crown and an aureola above, with ornaments forming red chains on both sides, and reddish-black, gradated face-tattooing). In one hand, the god waves three arrows or spears, in the other he holds a band somehow connected with the leaping fish and hung with trophy heads. These emblems, indispensable in ancient Peru, also hang at the sash surrounding the loins of the god. As in a mirror appears in these Paracas embroideries the ghostly fairyland of unknown, ancient Peruvian myths. And their blue resembles the sea, the realm of this god, like a dream which has become reality created by an artist of an unknown region of S. Peru over a thousand years ago and entombed in the Necropolis of Paracas. Ca. 300 to 600 A. D. Width of the embroidered panel: 12 cm.
Museum für Völkerkunde, Munich.
H. Hardt Collection.

NOTES ON THE PHOTOGRAPHS

1. Machu Picchu, Urubamba Valley, S. Peru. So-called House of the Three Windows. Whitish-grey granite. Trapeziform windows: Inca or Cuzco style. Height of middle window 1.30 m. In the background, the deep gorge of the Urubamba River. The mountain slopes partly covered by subtropical forests. Close to the upper margin of the picture, a snowy peak of the eastern Cordillera.

2. Machu Picchu, Urubamba Valley, S. Peru. Trapezium Gate in the 'Royal Group' of the buildings. Height 2.05 m. Above the gate, a large stone ring which was used – as were the bore holes right and left – for locking the gate by means of a wooden contrivance. Beyond the gate, a wall constructed of irregular megaliths. Whitish-grey granite.

3. Machu Picchu, Urubamba Valley, S. Peru. Trapezium Gates of Inca or Cuzco style in the 'Royal Group'. Whitish-grey granite.

4. Machu Picchu, Urubamba Valley, S. Peru. Wall with niches of precisely joined, regularly dressed blocks of light coloured granite. Height of niches 0.80 m. Between the recesses, quadrangular projections of a type which in other buildings apparently served to fix the roof. In the present case, as well as in the cave under the Torreón, this purpose is out of the question. Beyond the wall with recesses, and separated from it by a road, a wall of crudely hewn megaliths and smaller quarry-stones. From the right the shadow of the Torreón.

5. Machu Picchu, Urubamba Valley, S. Peru. To the left, buildings of the 'Royal Group' with staircase leading to the 'Torreón', a semi-circular tower, and to the beautiful wall with niches.

6. Machu Picchu, Urubamba Valley, S. Peru. The Torreón, erected on the top of a sacred rock, seen from below. The surface of the rock which is walled by the semi-circular Torreón has at various points been dressed into simple horizontal altar planes. Underneath the slanting, rising rock, there is a cave with high narrow trapezium niches (height 1.67 m.) and altar stones in the shape of steps hewn in the rock. This rock, with the Tor-reón surrounding it like a setting, is typical of the sacred rocks which for some reason or other were worshipped, presumably since prehistoric times, in the South American Highland (cp. also pls. 26–31). The often quoted 'apsis' of the Coricancha, the temple of the Sun in Cuzco, is constructed in a similar irregular curve (cp. H. Ubbelohde-Doering, *Auf den Königsstraßen der Inka*, pl. 170, text pp. 22–23). It is an open question, however, whether or not a sacred stone formed the centre of that curve in the Coricancha Golden Court.

7. Machu Picchu, Urubamba Valley, S. Peru. So-called House of the Altar. The altar, a large regular monolith of granite, measures 4.30 m. in length, 1.50 m. in height and 0.80 m. in depth. In the background the Intihuatana Rock.

8. Machu Picchu, Urubamba Valley, S. Peru. Left wall of the House of the Altar, built of large, regular monolithic slabs. The large slab on the left has a length of 3.16 m., a height of 2.43 m., and is 0.83 m. thick.

9. Machu Picchu, Urubamba Valley, S. Peru. So-called House of the Priest, behind the House of the Altar. Perfect regularity and harmony in the arrangement of the hewn stones. Example of the finest (early?) ashlar-work of the Incas.

10. Cuzco, ancient capital of the Inca Empire, S. Peru. Niche in the 'Temple Room of the Stars', Coricancha, Temple of the Sun (Golden Court). Classical example of the 'Inca' or 'Cuzco' niche. Height 72.5 cm., breadth 43.5 cm. below and 36.5 cm. above, depth 37 cm.

11. Cuzco. Masonry at the Apsis of the Temple of the Sun. The stones are worked to fit the curve of the wall as well as its incline.

12. Staircase and niche in the ruins of Tampu Machay near Cuzco, favourite residence, according to the tradition, of the Inca Tupac Yupanqui, and ancient sanctuary whose centre was perhaps a doubly lined fountain. Height of the niche 2.10 m., of the gate 3.50 m.

13. Cuzco. Wall of the Royal Palace of Inca Roca. Polygonal megalithic masonry from Cuzco's

ancient past. The prominences on the upper blocks right and left are explained as lugs for lifting-ropes or heavers not worked off afterwards.

14. The 'Fortress' of Sacsayhuaman near Cuzco. Triple zigzag wall, occupying the less steep slope of a hill above Cuzco. The writer believes that this was the sanctuary of an Inca royal clan, which in times of war could be defended like a fortress. The zigzag does not however point to a defensive purpose, as the same type of wall is found in sanctuaries unlikely to be interpreted as fortifications. Still, in ancient Peru, sanctuaries were places of defence *par excellence* and thereby took the character of fortresses; hence, perhaps, their designation as 'fortresses', often used by the chroniclers (cf. Tello and Kroeber in Kroeber, Peruvian Archaeology in 1942, Viking Fund Publications in Anthropology, 4, New York 1944, pp.46/47 and the corroborative remarks in a posthumous paper of Erland Nordenskiöld's Fortifications in Ancient Peru and Europe, Ethnos, vol. 7, No. 1, Stockholm, 1942). Early Cuzco Period.

15. Zigzag walls of the 'Fortress' of Sacsayhuaman near Cuzco. In the foreground, portions of the lowermost wall, the most powerful of the three walls. The huge corner-monolith at the right is about 5 m. high. The building rises like a citadel of the gods before the onlooker.

16. Corner-pillar in the lowermost zigzag wall of the Sacsayhuaman near Cuzco. Height about 5.5–6 m.

17. Megalithic zigzag walls with two gates. Sacsayhuaman near Cuzco. The monolith at the right of the lower gate measures 3.20 m. in height, 2.90 m. in breadth, and 2.15 m. in thickness. The upper gate belongs to the second, middle wall, and is shown in front view in the following plate.

18. Trapezium gate in the middle zigzag wall of the Sacsayhuaman near Cuzco. Clear space: height 3.50 m., lower breadth 1.55 m., upper breadth 1.10 m., depth 1.75 m.; lintel: 2.65 m. long, 0.75 m. high, 1.10 m. deep. Later than the lower zigzag wall. Whether and to what extent the oldest parts of the Sacsayhuaman are connected with the earliest Incas is a question that cannot safely be answered as long as the Early Inca Period and the position of Cuzco within that period present more problems than established facts. The same may be said of Ollantaytambo (pls. 20–24).

19. Small niche in a Sacsayhuaman wall facing the city of Cuzco. Honeycomb-like masonry. Period of Inca Tupac Yupanqui (?) (15th century A. D.).

20. Trapezium gate in a wall near Temple Hill on the Ollantaytambo mountain. Below the upper blocks, dislodged, presumably by some earthquake, are more narrow supporting blocks framed by two perfectly regular monoliths with notches such as those in the block on the following plate. The two gate pillars, too, look as though they were taken from the same mould, and in their mathematical regularity and the accuracy of the edges and corners resemble blocks of cast steel. The fact of their being dislodged makes the crystal-like shapes of the upper blocks appear more clearly. Reddish granite.

21. Shield-shaped block between two niches of the 'fortress' of Ollantaytambo, Urubamba Valley, S. Peru. Reddish granite. The notches on top – engaging the horizontal blocks –, characteristic of Cuzco architecture, are remarkably carefully and regularly worked. The two embossments below are considered devices facilitating heaving and transportation.

22. Symbolic ornament in relief on block IV. Height of portion shown, about 1.50 m.

23. Monoliths on Ollantaytambo Hill. In front, a transverse block at the edge of the uppermost terrace on which rises the Temple Hill. The edges of the blocks, particularly of the transverse one, are as straight and acute as in steel beams. The long ledge facilitating the transportation of the huge block has not been worked off. Dimensions of the block: 5.50 m. length, height 1.43 m., thickness 0.95.

In the background, Temple Hill with 6 monoliths standing upright towards the South East. Between these large monoliths are inserted narrow slabs that may have served to level out unevennesses of the monoliths' lateral faces.

The dimensions of the front monoliths are as follows (from left):

I. Height 3.50 m., breadth 1.65 m., thickness 1.15 m.

II. Height 3.40 m., breadth 1.35 m., thickness 1.10 m.

III. Height 3.90 m., breadth 1.30 m., thickness 0.70 m.

IV. Height 3.65 m., breadth 1.83 m., thickness 0.90 m.

V. Height 3.60 m., breadth 2.00 m., thickness 0.80 m.
(basal part is covered: breadth below 2.20 m. actual height about 3.80 m.).

VI. Height 4.05 m., breadth 1.90 m., thickness 1.80 m. (breadth below 2.16 m., thickness below 2.00 m.).

All of these monoliths are of reddish to flesh-coloured granite. The quarry whence were brought these blocks, weighing many tons each, is situated beyond the broad and deep Urubamba Valley, high up on the mountain slope (near the left margin of our picture). The monoliths, ready for use, had thus to be transported down to the valley, across the river, and uphill again. Quite a few have remained behind on the road (piedras cansadas, 'tired stones', as they are called).

24. Side-wall of the Temple hill of Ollantaytambo with large rectangular monolithic slabs lining rubble-work. In contrast to the masonry in front (see pl. 23), we have here before us the lesser accomplishments of later generations who, taking advantage of the huge dressed monoliths prepared by their forefathers, no longer knew how to join them correctly and therefore operated with rubble fillings.

25. Ruin of the so-called Viracocha Temple near Cacha, Vilcanota Valley, above Cuzco. One of the most uncommon buildings of the Southern Highland. A central brick wall on stone foundations, which today still has a height of 15 m., supported a gabled roof whose eaves rested on round brick pillars likewise founded on stone bases. In the background, part of the rear wall is visible.

The building may still belong in the earlier Inca Period: a definite date cannot as yet be assigned to it.

26. Wall with niches, surrounding the place for rites and festivals by the side of the 'Kenko'. The upper part of the wall down to the lintels of the niches has disappeared except for some stones in the background.

27. Sculptured rock 'Kenko' near Cuzco, showing step, altar-like platforms, chair-like seats, and winding offering-channels ('kenko' = that winds). To the left, a square for rites and festivals surrounded by a wall with niches (cp. the following plate). In the centre there are natural crevices leading toward a cave. This cave, which contains an imposing throne of a mummy (pl. 28) and thus takes the character of a shrine, is the very heart-piece of this rock. Possibly it was the sanctuary of one Ayllu, of a royal clan descended from an Inca ruler. Limestone.

28. Throne of the Dead in the 'Kenko' Cave. Hewn in the rock. Height 1.90 m. Behind the throne, deep dark clefts, realm of the dead. To the right and left and in the background, niches and altars carved in the rock.

29. Sculptured rock in front of the entrance to the cave called 'Choquequilla' ('Golden Moon') in the Huarocondo Gorge between the Pampa of Anta and Urubamba Valley, Cuzco region. The symbol of the steps recalls a similar formation in the "Bath of the Princess" near Ollantaytambo. Technically and in form of almost perfect beauty. Unfortunately, treasure hunters have dynamited the top part of the rock and thus mutilated one of the most noble works of ancient American art.

30. The sacred site of Concacha in the South Peruvian Highland between Cuzco and Abancay, with large sculptured monoliths: the 'Hill Stone' (pl. 31), on top of a natural hill that once by means of masonry now sunken in the ground had been given the shape of a pyramid in steps; at the foot of the hill, two 'Valley Stones', the larger of which is shown in our plate. This gigantic monolith is about 6 m. broad, and was split in the middle by a thunderbolt I was told. Sculptural treatment resembles that of the Kenko (see pl. 26 above), while the design as a whole suggests some architectural pattern, scene of religious cult and magic.

31. The 'Hill Stone' of Concacha in the mountains above Abancay. An ovoid boulder, 4.15 m. long, 3.10 m. broad, and 2.40 m. high, carved all over: teeming with figures of men and animals, jaguars or pumas, monkeys, snakes, vicunas (?), little temples with steps and terraces like a veritable mountain of gods. The stones of Concacha or Sayhuite are situated at almost 4000 m. above sea level.

32. Stone head, reported to be found in the vicinity of the Kenko above Cuzco. Height 35 cm. It appears to represent a member of one of the Inca royal clans, with the large ornamental ear discs as worn by Inca kinsfolk. The ovoid occipital elongation may be interpreted not as a particular deformation of the skull but as some sort of ceremonial headdress. A band in relief running over the forehead is reminiscent of the bands shown in the drawings of Inca rulers in Huaman Poma de Ayala's Chronicle, where they represent the 'llautu', the famous purple fringe, emblem and crown of the rulers (Huaman Poma de Ayala,

Nueva Corónica y buen gobierno: Institut d'Ethnologie, Travaux et Mémoires, Paris 1936, pp. 178, 324, 384.) The head was formerly covered with a whitish stucco, as evidenced by some remnants (nose, ear disc); traces of paint are not visible. The sculpture appears to belong to the time of the Spanish conquest or soon after.

33. Pan-pipe of stone (photo after a cast in the Museum für Völkerkunde, Berlin) with symbolical ornaments (reminiscent of ornaments on monoliths at Pucara and Hatuncolla). Height 13.5 cm. Present whereabouts of the original unknown. Inca culture, 13th to 16th centuries A. D.

34. Top: Alpacca of ice-grey stone with a yellowish hue. Libation cup. Length 12 cm. Region of Cuzco. Staatliches Museum für Völkerkunde, Munich, Collection of Spix and Martius, about 1820.
Bottom: Alpacca of black stone. Libation cup. Height 8 cm. Cuzco. Inca culture, 13th to 16th centuries A. D.
Norbert Mayrock Collection.

35. Top: Reclining Jaguar, carrying a round sacrificial bowl. Dark grey stone. Eyes, teeth, bristles and claws exhibit traces of ancient incrustations, partly with gold. Length 36 cm. South Peruvian Highland. Inca culture. 13th to 16th centuries A. D.
Prof. Bartels Collection, Dortmund.
Below: Stone Bowl with two handles, encircled by snakes whose heads rest on the margin and the handles of the bowl. Diameter 28 cm. Cuzco. Inca culture, 13th to 16th centuries A. D.
Berlin, Museum für Völkerkunde.

36. Large clay Amphora. Stylised panicles and delicate geometric ornaments painted in black on brown. Below the neck, an embossment shaped as a stylised jaguar-head which serves as a support to a rope when the vessel is carried. Conical bottom. Purest Inca or Cuzco-style: with the armies and officials advancing from Cuzco, this type is spread all over the country. Inca culture, 13th to 16th centuries A. D. Height 80 cm. Cuzco. H. and M. Gaffron Collection, Chicago.

37. Small Cuzco Amphora. Height 23 cm. A snake in relief winds around the neck and down the wall. Traces of a white slip without paint. Inca culture, 13th to 16th centuries A. D.
Museum für Völkerkunde, Munich.

38. Large Clay Vessel, with gracefully drawn figures of dancing skeletons wearing loose garments with step patterns (cp. the cloak pl. 46). Colouring of the dancers: white, yellow, orange, black. The ground in brownish-crimson. Height 39 cm., Abancay, South Peruvian Highland. Inca culture, 13th to 16th centuries A. D.
Museum für Völkerkunde, Munich; presented by Dr. Bergeat.

39. Cup with handle. Painted with plant-like ornaments above, geometric ornaments below. The boxed rectangles possibly symbolize the gate of the earth, the cave whence man came and to which after death he returns according to the highlander's belief. (cf. H. Ubbelohde-Doering, *Auf den Königsstraßen der Inka*, pp. 27/29).
A cave of this kind is the interior of the Kenko rock above Cuzco (see plate 27 and explanations given there). The handle, by virtue of the head placed on it, has become the body of a feline beast. Height 12.5 cm. Colouring: white, red, black. Cuzco. Inca culture, 13th to 16th centuries A. D. Norbert Mayrock Collection.

40. Above: Clay Dish with two loop-handles. The geometric painting (meant symbolically) is akin to that on the cup in pl. 39. Shape and decor typical of Inca or Cuzco, respectively. Pale yellow body; the framing lozenges red; the star-crosses grey-yellow; the small rectangles red. Handles decorated with a simple wicker-work pattern. Diameter 19 cm, inclusive of handles. Island of the sun, Lake Titicaca. Inca culture. 13th to 16th centuries A. D.
Museum für Völkerkunde, Munich.
Bottom: Small clay vessel with painted black birds on dull, yellow ground. Loop handle with basket weave ornament, similar to the dish on top. Diameter 13 cm. Cuzco, Inca culture, 13th to 16th centuries A. D.

41. Flat Dish, painted with red fishes in black outlines and black tadpoles on white ground. The idea is not to depict nature, but to conjure water by way of the representative symbols, fish and tadpole. Interspersed are black fruits (pepper-pods ?). Knob-handle with painted wicker-work patterns. Shape typical of Inca-Cuzco style; painting under influence of the Nazca style. Problem: the dish was found in the Nazca region; the Nazca culture however, according to our present knowledge, came to an end at a period more than 500 years before the Incas occupied the Nazca valleys. We ought to surmise therefore, that Nazca style elements lingered on throughout that long span

of time, while other powerful cultures swept, wave after wave, over the Nazca valleys. An assumption that sounds rather unlikely and at the same time offers an example of the difficulties encountered time and again by archaeological research in Peru. Diameter 23.4 cm., inclusive of handle. Nazca Valleys, S. Peru.

H. and M Gaffron Collection, Chicago. (Two comparable, smaller dishes are in the Museum für Völkerkunde, Berlin; cf. Lehmann-Doering, *Kunstgeschichte des alten Peru*, pl. 96).

42. Top: Llama; chased silver sheets, pieced together, with golden ornament at the back. Height 23.2 cm. From the Sun Island, Titicaca Lake. Inca culture, 13th to 16th centuries A. D. American Museum of Natural History, New York. (cf. Bandelier, *Island of Titicaca and Coati*, pl. LVIII).

Bottom: Llama; chased silver sheets, pieced together. Height 22.9 cm. From the Sun Island, Titicaca Lake. Inca culture, 13th to 16th centuries A. D.

American Museum of Natural History, New York.

43. Statuette of a woman, chased silver. Of extraordinary size: 15 cm., as against an average size of only a few centimetres. Statuettes of this kind were, as a rule, wrapped in garments like dolls, so that only the head was seen. From the Sun Island, Titicaca Lake. Inca culture, 13th to 16th centuries A. D.

Museum für Völkerkunde, Munich.

44. Silver dish with inlaid red and lilac shell and green stone (malachite?). Diam. (with handle) 19.5 cm. Found on the sculptured rock Titicaca near Cuzco, in a depth of 40 cm. Typical Cuzco-(Inca-) style. Inca-culture, 13th to 16th century A. D.

45. Gold Statuette of a woman. Provenance: Hualla-Hualla near Lauramarca, Cuzco-region, S. Peru. Typical Inca-Cuzco style. Inca culture, 13th to 16th centuries A. D. Height of the statuette 24.5 cm., weight 524 gr.

Museo de Arqueología, Cuzco.

46. Large Fabric, with colourful embroidery showing groups of birds in five step-sided panels. Put together, the four corner-panels would result in a figure similar to the central panel. At the narrow sides, borders consisting of an inner row of densely placed fishes and an outer row of equally densely placed feathers. The shroud itself is a simple cotton fabric that has assumed a dark brown

colour and is very decayed; originally, its colour presumably was white. The pattern is of wool. Length 280 cm., breadth 200 cm. Los Majuelos, Valley of the Rio Grande de Nazca, S. Peru. Inca culture, 13th to 16th centuries A. D. Museum für Völkerkunde, Munich.

47. Detail – 2/3 of natural size – from a large and heavy woollen blanket in Gobelin technique. In chessboard order, multicoloured stars (with colour alternating in a regular scheme), stylised birdheads separated by diagonal stripes, and more rarely zigzag bands. The very large blanket displays also several small figures of llamas, arranged irregularly. The ground in deep rubyred. Nazca Valleys (?), S. Peru. Inca culture, 13th to 16th centuries A. D.

H. and M. Gaffron Collection, Chicago.

48. Fine woollen veil in brilliant colours, changing in triangles in ritual alternation. The fabric does not consist of warp and weft as normally found, but of many small units with their particular warp and weft, and apparently was composed by means of some auxiliary net ('Netzkettentechnik'). Red, yellow, orange, blue, green. Width 97 cm. Length of the veil 1,90 m. Nazca Valley, S. Peru. Inca culture, 13th to 14th centuries A. D. or earlier.

Museum für Völkerkunde, Munich.

49. Fragment of a cloak of Llama or Alpaca wool. Llama figures are woven in, in faint greyish yellow on black and brown ground. Nazca-Region. Inca culture, 13th–16th century A. D. Height of decorated strip 14 cm.

Museum für Völkerkunde, Munich.

50. Cloak. Gobelin fabric with chequer pattern in black and white framing a broad wedge-shaped portion in a brilliant ruby colour. On both sides and below, most noticeably around the edges of the sleeves and at the lower border, the cloak is decorated with threads in many colours: a feature characteristic of Inca fabrics. So is the chequer pattern, which often appears in the book of Huaman Poma de Ayala, although it should be noted that, to judge from vase paintings, the same pattern was common in the short cloaks or shirts of warriors of the period of the Mochica culture which flourished some centuries before the rise of the Inca culture. The ancient Nazca culture, too, has provided instances of the black and white chequers in garments depicted on vessels, instances that again take us – reckoning from the

time of our Inca weaver's cloak – well over half a millenium back in time, so that we face once more the puzzle touched upon under no. 41 above. Length 95 cm.; breadth 78 cm. Material: Warp, cotton; weft, wool. Los Majuelos, Valley of the Rio Grande de Nazca, S. Peru. Inca culture, 13th to 16th centuries A. D. From the same tomb came the large fabric, pl. 47.
Museum für Völkerkunde, Munich.

51. Feather Cloak. Above on white ground, two black pumas (?) with red mouths; below them three birds: right and left, grey with red feet; middle, black with blue feet; in the lower row, two black birds with greenish feet and two stepped symbols in grey with red design. Border: step-sided frets – a universally applied ornament of ancient Peruvian art – with steps or wings in black and red. Size: 85 × 85 cm. Nazca Valley, S. Peru. Inca culture, 13th to 16th centuries A. D.
H. and M. Gaffron Collection, Chicago.

52. Tower of the Lizard (named after a relief on its outer wall, see following plate). One of the so-called sepulchral-towers, 'Chullpas', at Sillustani, Umayo Lake, Titicaca basin, about 3900 m. above sea-level. The Tower is not cylindrical but tapers toward the base, so that the upper part with the cornice protrudes over the foot. To secure in this construction the assemblage of the very accurately joined stones, these were 'bolted', as it were, by means of round pebbles in a loam bedding, filling semi-circular cavities of adjoining squares. In the interior of the tower, a narrow chamber with a sham vault. Height of the tower, about 9 m. So-called 'Chullpa-Colla' culture; chronological position not definitely ascertained; perhaps 10th to 13th centuries A. D.

53. Tower of the Lizard, Sillustani, Umayo Lake. Outer wall. (cp. the preceding plate).

54. Ruined City of Chanchán, near Trujillo, N. Peruvian coast. Air view. The spacious rectangles, partly doubly walled, are the so-called palaces. In the background, at the right, pyramids, destroyed by treasure hunters. Near the lower edge, pillaged grave-yards of early periods. The ruins cover several square kilometres. Chanchán was the residence of the Gran Chimú, ruler of the Chimú kingdom, 12th to 15th century A. D. Defeated by the Inca around 1450 A. D. and subsequently incorporated into the Inca Empire.

55. Mural Reliefs in the 'Hall of Arabesques', Chanchán (cp. plate 54). Typifying the transla-tion of textile pattern into architectural decoration, here executed in an 'alloy' of clay and some sort of cement on brick walls. It is likely that these reliefs were once painted. (As an example of a translation of tapestries into stone, cp. the Sun Gate at Tiahuanaco, pl. 122).
Bottom: Rhomboid wall reliefs with fishes moving around water-fowl. Huaca Esmeralda, near Chanchán. Chimú culture. 12th to 15th centuries A. D.

56. Left: Fragment of a ceremonial spear, in a 'holy lance', of hard dark-brown Huarango wood. Carved figures in six superposed zones separated, in the middle, by a wavy band. The winged figure above the wavy band has a 'speech scroll' terminated by an animal's head. (In ancient Peru, these 'speech scrolls' occur with figures in Coastal Tiahuanaco art.) The crescent in the crown of this divine being, on the other hand, is strongly reminiscent of crowns of warriors, gods, and demons in vase paintings of the Mochica culture. The fragment, hailing from the Lambayeque area, may thus belong to the 10th to 12th centuries A. D. and perhaps be still coeval with the beginning of the Chimú culture. Length 63,5 cm.
Right: Large, flat socket of hammered gold-sheets, with chased bird-figures. Perforations along the left edge in order to fasten threads. Length 35 cm. Region of Lambayeque, N. Peru. Chimú culture, 14th to 15th centuries A. D.
Museum für Völkerkunde, Hamburg. E. Brüning Collection.

57. Black Clay Bottle. On the shoulder, a relief of jagged angular spirals on granulated ground, and a monkey figure snuggling in the bend between handle and spout. Height 23 cm. Shape and decoration typical of the pottery of the Chimú culture, 14th to 15th centuries A. D. Chanchán area, N. Peru.
H. and M. Gaffron Collection, Chicago.

58. Upper left: Blackish-grey Clay Vessel in the shape of a raft of rushes steered by two men. They operate with oars of a type known from tombs at the northern coast. Close to the base of the spout, on the 'stirrup', which is handle and spout in one, there is a little crouching monkey. Monkey figures placed that way are traditional with the late Chimú culture. Height 22,5 cm. Chanchán area? N. Peruvian coast. 12th to 15th centuries A. D.
Coll. H. and M. Gaffron, Chicago.

Upper right: Clay Vessel in the shape of a pumpkin. Grey-black with whitish incrustations. Height 23 cm. N. Peruvian coast near Chanchán? Chimú culture, 12th to 15th centuries A. D. Museum für Völkerkunde, München.

Bottom: Black Clay Vessel with two long, slender, tapering spouts between which rises a jagged arch with zigzag ornaments in openwork. This arch reveals itself as the body of a double-headed snake whose heads issue from the bases of the spouts. From their mouths emanate what appear to be their tongues, which however may have to be interpreted as 'speech scrolls', as Tiahuanaco style affinities in these heads would suggest. The arched snake with its two heads calls to mind the two-headed heavenly snake of the Mochica paintings.

On the apex of the arch, there is the head of a god which likewise exhibits Tiahuanaco style elements. Four small frogs on the shoulder of the pot have their eyes fixed upon the lord on top of the arch, as though they were expecting his orders. As in Ancient Peru the frog often appears as a symbol of rain, the personage on top may well represent the lord of heavenly waters whose will is carried out by the frogs.

Height 17.5 cm. Example of the late style of Lambayeque region, N. Peru, about 12th to 14th centuries A. D. Coll. H. and M. Gaffron, Chicago.

59. Raft of rushes with two oarsmen. Cast silver. The oars like planks (cp. pl. 58 upper left). The strange high hats the men wear recall tassels such as occur in late textiles from the N. Peruvian coast. Between the two round-eyed men whose dauntless yet apprehensive faces recount the dangers in their extremely small craft, there lies a sizeable fish, reward of their venture. A rare object of great charm in its formal and technical treatment. Chicama Valley, N. Peru. Chimú culture, 12th to 15th centuries A. D.
Private Collection.

60. Sacrificial knife of an alloy of copper and gold. The place of the handle is taken by the figure of a god in a sumptuous garment, with small wings at his upper arms. He wears a crown of enormous size decorated with snakes. The birds suspended at the lower edge of the crown, too, are not simply ornaments but have some particular meaning. Height 43.5 cm. From a treasure discovered in 1937 at Illimo, Department of Lambayeque, N. Peruvian coast. (Cp. plate 61.)

Early Chimú culture, 12th to 13th Centuries A. D. or earlier.
Museo Nacional de Arqueología, Lima.

61. Top: Chased goblets of an alloy of gold and copper. Round and angular pearled frames hold – or held – inlays of turquoise which in part are lost. Below the rim, a frieze of winged or stepped hooks: one of the ubiquitous symbols of ancient Peru. Near the bases of the goblets there are small ledges. These mark a second bottom, let in to create hollow spaces serving as magic rattles. Height 15.5 cm. From the Illimo Treasure, Lambayeque area, N. Peru. (Cp. plate 60.) 12th to 13th centuries A. D. or earlier.
Museo Nacional de Arqueología, Lima.

Bottom: Another three goblets of a gold-copper alloy from the Illima Treasure (see plates 60 to 61), adorned with chased figures of gods. The heads of these figures recall that on top of the heavenly snake of the vessel in plate 58 (below). Height 21 cm. (cf. L. Valcárcel, in Revista del Museo Nacional, Lima 1937, VI, p. 164 ff.). Early Chimú culture, 12th to 13th centuries A. D. or earlier.
Museo Nacional de Arqueología, Lima.

62. Upper left: Flexible golden goblet with figures of animals hammered out in relief. They fill the space between the traditional frieze of winged or stepped hooks (a symbol of clouds?) above and the bulging zones below as though they were hovering between heaven and earth. Height 9.5 cm. Lambayeque, N. Peru. Chimú culture, 12th to 15th centuries A. D.
Museum für Völkerkunde, Munich.

Upper right: Golden spatula (for lime powder chewed with coca-leaves) with bird; length 5.7 cm. Golden needle with vulture-like bird; length 12.3 cm. Both pieces from the Northern coast. Chimú-culture, 12th to 15th century A. D.
Norbert Mayrock Collection.

Below left: Golden, spiral tweezers, with handle in the shape of a bird of prey. Northern coast. Chimú-culture, 12th to 15th century. A. D.
Norbert Mayrock Collection.

63. Top: Golden Ear-Disc, shaped as a shallow bowl with a broad pearled rim, that frames the figure of a bird. Wrought of gold sheets, this vulture or falcon-like creature looks almost like a bird in medieval heraldry. Diameter 4.7 cm. Cerro Zapamé near Lambayeque, N. Peru. Early Chimú culture, 12th to 13th centuries A. D.

Museum für Völkerkunde, Hamburg; E. Brüning Collection.

Bottom: Golden Ear-Disc with pearled rim encircling the figure of a god in ornate attire, very similar to the figures in the goblets on plate 62 (upper left) and in the knife on plate 60. In his right hand, the god holds a slender golden tumbler; with his left he brandishes a rattle. Diameter 10 cm. Lambayeque region; possible from Cerro Zapamé. Early Chimú culture, 12th to 13th centuries A. D.

Museum für Völkerkunde, Hamburg; E. Brüning Collection.

64. Top: Jaguar, gold, chased and soldered. The eyes and the mouth may originally have held some inlay. Length 11 cm. Lambayeque, N. Peru. Early Chimú culture, 12th to 13th centuries A. D. Norbert Mayrock Collection.

(An almost identical piece in the Museum für Völkerkunde, Hamburg; E. Brüning Collection).

Bottom: Two small Jaguar-masks of hammered gold-sheets. They appear to have been incrusted with shell and semi-precious stones (?). Small perforations along the edges permitted the mask to be sewn on to clothes or ceremonial dress. Height: left 4.1 cm. Lambayeque region, N. Peru. Early Chimú culture, 12th to 13th centuries A. D. or earlier.

Museum für Völkerkunde, Hamburg; E. Brüning Collection.

65. Top: At the left, a dancer (?) wearing a stag-mask and almost hidden under his pompous drapery. In the middle, a personage from Lilliput who, defying the weight of his crown and the standards (? or wings) on his back, dances towards the right while swinging a small drum. At the right, a spider, crowned and hence exalted to a divine sphere, with eight eggs arranged in two rows. These three figures are wrought of gold sheets. Sizes: mask-bearer 4.8 cm. high; dancer with drum 4.5 cm.; spider about 4.8 cm. long. We know nothing of the myths upon which these representations are based. Cerro Zapamé near Lambayeque, N. Peru. Aarly Chimú culture, 12th to 13th centuries A. D.

Museum für Völkerkunde, Hamburg; E. Brüning Collection.

Bottom: Two golden scorpion-beings wearing broad crowns which – as insignia of the gods – indicate their celestial character. Height: left 4.5 cm., right 2.8 cm. Cerro Zapamé near Lam-

bayeque, N. Peru. Early Chimú culture, 12th to 13th centuries A. D.

Museum für Völkerkunde, Hamburg; E. Brüning Collection.

66. Pole-top of cast copper with some light-green verdigris. On top of a cylindrical piece adorned by a very realistic pattern of twisted ropes running slantingly, there is a birf-figure in the round. The bird, whose tail is terminated by a kind of tassel similar to those occurring in Chimú textiles, has swooped down upon a snake winding on the ground. Impressive piece of Old Peruvian metal sculpture. Height 15.5 cm. Chimú culture, 12th to 15th centuries A. D.

Norbert Mayrock Collection.

67. Bowl, made of the base of a gourd which on the outer side is blackened and decorated with figures inlaid in colourful shell and malachite-green stones. A frieze of gods with big ceremonial crowns and with goblets in their raised hands surrounds the figure of a demonic scorpion(?) occupying the centre of the bottom. The head of this demon reminds one of similar heads in the art of the Mochica culture. The telescoped triangles or cones rising from the lateral tips of the crowns, on the other hand, are a feature known from ceremonial staffs, apparel, and a peculiar throne of the Chimú culture. The bowl will therefore have to be assigned to either early Chimú – 12th to 13th centuries A. D. – or a culture that immediately preceded it. Provenance: Paramonga area. The rim of the bowl, except for the spot the lips touch (rear centre in the lower picture), is adorned by small discs of shell. Diametre 16.5 cm.

Norbert Mayrock Collection.

68. Detail of a tapestry with design in relief of animal skins between which are arranged figures of animals, birds, and flowering plants. Suze of portion shown: 54×23 cm. Size of the whole fabric: 89×35 cm. Pachacamac (?), Middle Peruvian coast. After 1000 A. D.

H. and M. Gaffron Collection, Chicago.

69. Short cloak. The fabric is covered all over by woollen threads which produce a pelt-like texture and form the background of plastic figures in needlework. These figures, stuffed with cotton, represent gods of anthropomorphous appearance, standing under canopies or crowing aureoles and being escorted by condor-like attendants. Colours: light red ground; decor in yellow, white, blue, pink, brown, and black. Along the lower border,

a festoon of heavy tassels issuing from small demon-heads in needlework. Overlapping the festoon, a large tassel composed of needleworked flowers, leaves, and roots, ending in woollen tassels. One of the most fantastic works of ancient Peruvian textile art ever known. Length (both sides) 100 cm., breadth 87 cm.
North Peruvian coast. Chimú culture 12th to 15th centuries A. D.
The Brooklyn Museum, Brooklyn. Courtesy of the Museum.

70. Portion of a very large veil-like fabric with blue and brown bird-figures printed on it. Size of portion shown: 150 × 150 cm. Size of the whole fabric 300 × 340 cm. Pacasmayo area, N. Peru. Chimú culture, 12th to 15th centuries A. D.
Private Collection.

71. Double-weaving in red and white: The woven patterns appear on the one side in red on white, on the other, in white on red. Size of portion shown 42 × 30 cm.; size of the whole cloak 64 × 55 cm. Pachacamac, Central Peruvian Coast. About 11th to 12th centuries. A. D.
Museum für Völkerkunde, Berlin.

72. Large clay Urn in the shape of a human being with a libation cup in his hands. Yellowish white and dark brown. Height 52 cm. Chancay. About 12th to 15th centuries A. D.
Museum für Völkerkunde, Munich.

73. Left: Large clay goblet with chocolate-coloured decor on white slip. Small twisted loop for suspension (?). Height 23.5 cm. Chancay. About 12th to 15th centuries A. D.
Museum für Völkerkunde, Munich.
Right: Large clay urn with dark-brown *décor* on off-white ground. The checker board pattern is commonly found in ancient Peruvian art and ranges from the Mochica aud Paracas culture to the Inca culture. Height 48 cm. Chancay, about 12th–15th century A. D.
Museum für Völkerkunde, Munich.

74. Two silver cups, said to have been found in the Armatambo ruins near Chorillos, a sea-resort south from Lima. The form of the vessel to the right with its graded zones occurs among gold tumblers hailing from Ica Valley, S. Peru (H. and M. Gaffron Collection; cf. Heinrich U. Doering, *Altperuanische Kunst*, Berlin 1936, pl. 41 top). Height of the left cup 10 cm, of the right one 13.5 cm. About 12th to 15th centuries A. D.
Museum für Völkerkunde, Munich.

75. Fragment of a tapestry showing pattern of branches with leaves in dull green on whitish ground. Outlines reworked after weaving. It would appear that, whole and undamaged, this fabric, a large blanket or hanging such as were used also in draperied tombs (e. g., in the Nazca Valleys), was among the most exquisite of Ancient Peruvian textiles. Size 29 × 45.5 cm. Pachacamac. After 1000 A. D.
Museum für Völkerkunde, Berlin.

76. Tapestry magical fish in soft, subdued shades of blue and light brown. The whole of the surface displays a great variety of symbols which, however abbreviated, undoubtedly were understood in their time as readily as hieroglyphs, while to us their significance is still unknown. Light star-crosses are strewn over the head and the body of the fish as though it had passed through a rain of stars or the phosphorescent sea and were still reflecting their cold fires. Application on a larger piece of ivory coloured cotton. Size: 49 × 27.5 cm. Pachacamac. After 1000 A. D.
Museum für Völkerkunde, Berlin; presented by H. and M. Gaffron.

77. Tapestry with design of plants with roots, leaves, and ruby-red flowers, applied on a loose fabric. Due to bitumen-like dye, perhaps containing humic acid, the dark brown parts of the tapestry filling the spaces between the stalks and branches are destroyed. Size 39 × 16 cm. Pachacamac. After 1000 A. D.
H. and M. Gaffron Collection, Chicago.

78. Veil in batik technique with undyed design of flower stalks. At the left, tapestry border with plastic embroidery. Length 60.5 cm. Pachacamac. After 1000 A. D.
H. and M. Gaffron Collection, Chicago.

79. Veil-fabric showing design in batik technique of a flowering plant on coloured ground. Length 40 cm. Pachacamac. After 1000 A. D.
H. and M. Gaffron Collection, Chicago.

80. Tapestry looking like a framed picture. Represented are stylised plants (corn with cobs and enveloping leaves?) with (abbreviated) birds flying around; above the plants (= behind them), a phantom animal prowls and, around the roots, fishes swim. The picture contains all that was necessary for the life of Old Peruvian peasants: water, symbolized by fishes; fruit and food, symbolized by the corn – and the birds, which appear when the corn ripens, and the more so

if the harvests are abundant. The feline or fox-like animal remains uninterpreted, but surely it has its significance within the whole of the picture. There can be no doubt that the meaning embodied in the fabric was the reason why it was made; weaving in itself may have been a magical performance that either conjures or exorcises. The belief of the makers was that their desires – as expressed in the magically effective image of their weavings – would be fulfilled through the good offices of their dead when these had passed into the other, supernatural life. The border with abbreviations of animal figures that seem to rotate round the heads placed in their centres, is likely to correspond some way or other to the picture it frames. Size 33×35 cm. Pachacamac. Central Peruvian Coast. After 1000 A. D.
H. and M. Gaffron Collection, Chicago.

81. Part of a fine tapestry with design of many figures, a kind of textile characteristic of the later Pacha-camac production. The pictures appear to be narrative in character, but what they narrate is hardly anything in the way of historical events but mythical doings, represented regardless of time and space. The roundel in the lower qua-drangle, which shows a circle of dancers encom-passed by a fringe of rolling waves to which a similar fringe in the centre answers, makes one think of Coptic textiles. If such were mixed with comparable ones from Peru, it would not be easy even for a connoisseur to decide at first glance the respective provenance. Length 28 cm. Total length 41 cm. Pachacamac. After 1000 A. D.
Museum für Völkerkunde, Munich; Heinrich Hardt Collection.

82. Picture of a fruit-tree, painted on white cotton fabric. Remarkably powerful outlines. Marquez. After 1000 A. D.
Museum für Völkerkunde, Berlin.

83. Large woollen veil with pattern of interlaced S-shaped snakes in yellow and red on brown ground, separated by bands of white squares. 'Plangi' dyeing technique: the squares to be left white are first covered to stay clear of the dyestuff, after which the whole fabric is dyed yellow; then the squares to remain yellow are protected and the fabric is dyed brown. When, after drying, the covering squares are removed, the pattern in its several colours emerges. The fringe is made of unspun ruby-red wool. Among the symbols cur-rent in Ancient Peru, that of the S-curved snake

stands out. These S-shaped snakes represent, in my opinion, magical images of the lightning and all that it implies: the thunderstorm, the rain in the mountains, and the waters thence coming down and bringing fertility to the land along the coast. We thus might describe the fabric as truly charged with lightning; waved about like an Aegis it might unleash a thunderstorm and cause rain to pour down. Size 105×235 cm. Paramonga. After 1000 A. D.
Museum für Völkerkunde, Munich.

84. Clay bowls with geometrical ornaments derived, apparently, from basketry patterns. An affinity to basketry shapes is revealed also by the fact that the rim of the lower pot is everted as in a basket. Around the carinated zone this pot is further decorated by a frieze of small birds con-trasting with the basketry character of the rest. Height: upper bowl 9.8 cm.; lower bowls 6.5 cm. each. Ica Valley, S. Peruvian coast.
14th to 15th centuries A. D.
Museum für Völkerkunde, Berlin.

85. Large *repoussé* gold tumbler in the shape of a rigidly stylised head with aquiline nose – typical of this kind of gold or silver vessel from the Ica Valley. Regarding form, the head appears to depend on prototypes carved in wood. Height 17 cm. Ica Valley. About 13th to 15th centuries A. D. H. and M. Gaffron Collection, Chicago.

86. Bracelet; chased and hammered gold sheet. The *décor* consists of vertically superposed triangular human heads; in the centre, small birds looking left and right take the place of the heads in the lower half. Height 11 cm. Ica Valley, S. Peru. 13th to 15th centuries A. D.
Sutorius Collection.

87. Heavy gold bracelet with bosses in *repoussé* technique. Height 15.5 cm. Ica Valley, S. Peru. 13th to 15th centuries A. D.
Museum für Völkerkunde, Munich.

88. Fabric embroidered with small coloured deer figures. Length of portion shown 30 cm.
H. and M. Gaffron Collection, Chicago.

89. Cloak of tapestry, the slits mostly sewn. Pattern of interlocked angular hooks in black and golden yellow. The hooks have the usual annex of wings or steps. Alternately red and black birds of real-istic design occupy the yellow wings, while the black wings and hooks are filled with rows of very small birds, pictographically abbreviated. In regard to both colouring and design, one of the

most beautiful pieces among the later textiles from Old Peru. The slit for the neck (middle of the left edge in our reproduction) here runs transversely, from shoulder to shoulder, while usually it runs lengthwise. Size 60×85 cm. Nazca Valleys, S. Peru. About 1000 A. D. or later.
Museum für Völkerkunde, Munich.

90. Veil fabric, *à-jour* technique, with bird-figures arranged in rows between wave-bands running slantwise. Old Peruvian textile workers excelled in making decorated veils in various techniques. Peruvian coast. After 1000 A. D.
The Brooklyn Museum, Brooklyn. Courtesy of the Museum.

91. Large goblet of chased gold with two bulging belts. Height 13 cm. Pachacamac (?). (cf. Baessler, Altperuanische Metallgeräte). About 1000 A.D.
Private Collection.

92. Small Cloak in a delicate Gobelin technique, with woven, multi-coloured birds. The wedge-shaped conformation framed by small colourful squares and filled with figures might be suggestive of a date as late as Inca or of an assignment to some coeval culture in the Nazca Valleys; the same is true for the coloured borders of the little cloak. However, the rectangular fields at the lower fringe with exceedingly delicately rendered birds, which look almost like painted miniatures, rather recall earlier styles, such as that of the expiring Coastal Tiahuanaco culture toward the 11th to 12th centuries, when considerable changes of its artistic aspect had taken place. This date is favoured also by several figurative potteries distinctly tiahuanacoid in character, potteries said to have come from the same tomb where the little cloak was found. Size 78×64 cm. Atarco, Taruga Valley, Nazca Region, S. Peru.
Museum für Völkerkunde, Munich.

93. Top: Clay Bottle seen from above, with brightly painted two slender spouts connected by a handle. On its upper face, two painted heads of demonic beasts. From their mouth emerge bands looking like 'speech-scrolls'. Height 8.5 cm. Coastal Tiahuanaco culture, between 700 and 900 A. D., Nazca region.
Museum für Völkerkunde, Munich.
Bottom: Two needle-cases of reed, lined with a pattern fabric in which the warp is replaced by very thinly split reeds. The weft is woollen in various dyes. Figures in Coastal Tiahuanaco style. Lids of wood, fastened through perforations to plated cords. Length of the case in front 14 cm. Nazca Valleys, S. Peru. Coastal Tiahuanaco culture, about 700 to 900 A. D.
Museum für Völkerkunde, Munich.

94. Thick-walled clay goblet, painted in Tiahuanaco style ('Coastal Tiahuanaco'). The god represented is the same as that in the frieze of the Tiahuanaco Sun Gate: with quadrangular head, squarish teeth, and body stiff, like ashlarwork. Height 10.5 cm. Pachacamac near Lima, Central Peruvian Coast. Coastal Tiahuanaco culture, about 700–900 A. D.
Norbert Mayrock Collection.

95. Two clay bowls, painted with figures of winged animal demons in Tiahuanaco style. Lacquer-like surface. Colours above: yellow, red, grey; below: white, yellow, grey. Diameter above: 12 cm., below: 11.5 cm. Nazca Valleys, S. Peru. Coastal Tiahuanaco culture about 700 to 900 A. D.
Norbert Mayrock Collection.

96. Mummy mask with shell-incrusted eyes. Wide open, beaming, startling eyes, gazing demoniacally; intensified by long and dense lashes of black hair which at the upper lids is glued into the resinous substance that holds the white shell eyes in place. Traces of red colour would seem to indicate that the head was painted red all over. Red was the cardinal colour in ancient Peru especially for the cult of the dead. In this and in its whole physiognomy, the head can be likened to the well-known heads from Pacheco, those 'pièces de résistance' of ancient Peruvian art. Unquestionably there must have existed connections between the Pacheco heads, the present head from Pachacamac, the gorgeous tombac mask from Moche (pl. 230), and several formations within the iconography of Chavín (cf. my study on 'Tonplastik aus Nazca', Ipek, 1927, pp. 67 ff.). The mask appears to have been adorned with a crown of metal (copper, silver, or gold) or a turban. Pachacamac, Central Peruvian coast. Coastal Tiahuanaco culture, about 700 to 900 A. D.
Museum für Völkerkunde, Berlin.

97. Top: Much enlarged condor-head from one of the choicest fabrics in Tiahuanaco style; displays, on the one hand, the technique under a magnifying glass, while on the other hand it makes evident the monumental form latent in even the smallest Tiahuanaco style figure. Original size of the head only 2.3×3.5 cm.! The vicuña wool used in this

fabric looks like the finest silk, while the woven images, not enlarged, seem like miniature paintings. (Size of the whole fragment 1.35 × 1.08 m). Nazca Valleys S. Peru. Coastal Tiahuanaco culture, about 700 to 900 A. D.

Bottom: Part of the fabric given above. This section shows a demon turning to the right, with condor-head (middle right), human legs and feet (middle left and upper left corner), narrow wings (upper right corner), crown (between wings and head), and large sceptre ending in two fish-heads (whole lower section) and held in the demon's hand (lower middle). Length of the figure: 15 cm. Museum für Völkerkunde, Munich. Presented by Norbert Mayrock.

98. Part of a tapestry cloak. Between plain ruby faces, a panel decorated with figures in pairs. On account of its skull and the rendering of arm-bones and leg-bones, one of the figures can be explained as a death-spirit. The other one, carrying bow and arrow, might be taken as a living warrior were it not for the tip of the nose that looks as if incrusted and the teeth-grinning mouth, features demanding a different interpretation, viz., as a god or a demon. Possibly, we here have to do with pairs of gods or semi-gods, one of them being a winged god of death, while the other one, in great ceremonial attire with winged eye and the 'trail of tears' below it, may be his opposite, a being still unknown to us, that embodies the supernatural world. In both of these configurations, none of the numerous symbols of which they are composed is negligible or just decorative, and the tiniest detail could as little be dispensed with as in a fugue of Bach's. Colours: framing borders in a brilliant ruby, ground of middle stripe, a golden ochre. In the death-god as in the archer-god, an 'Apollo' of ancient Peru, interchange: red, yellow, orange, brown, black, white and grey. Worthy of note is the fact that the skeleton god is one-footed, as the other leg ends in an animal head. The archer, too, shows a condor-head attached to his foot, while the foot itself is not lacking. This feature of the death-god must on no account be considered as a creation of the weaver's fancy. As with everything in these ancient Peruvian tapestries, the lack of a foot and substitution by an animal head must have some meaning. In this connection I should like to point out a conspicuous parallel to these woven images: a painted pair

of gods on leaves 56 and 73 of the Old-Mexican Borgia Codex where, as in the present case, the two figures appear back to back. They are the death-god, Mictlantecutli, and the wind-god, Quetzalcouatl (cf. E. Seler, Kommentar IV, pls., Codex Borgia). Breadth of the portion shown: about 40 cm. Necropolis of Ancón, Central Peruvian Coast, North of and near to Lima. Coastal Tiahuanaco culture, about 700 to 900 A. D. Museum für Völkerkunde, Berlin.

99. Portion of a ruby-red cloak in Gobelin technique, with multi-coloured complexes of symbols: frontally rendered jaguar-heads in pairs (middle of broad stripe), pairs of condor-heads (at the margins of the stripes), pairs of corn-cobs (between border and middle of the broad stripe and in the narrow stripe), and other symbols, the significance of which is unknown. Colours: black, white, gold-ochre, red, apple-green, and turquoise. Size of the cloak 110 × 104 cm.; size of the portion shown about 80 × 58 cm. Nazca Valleys, S. Peru. Coastal Tiahuanaco culture, about 700 to 900 A. D. H. and M. Gaffron Collection, Chicago.

100. Miniature Cloak in Gobelin technique, showing animal-headed demons who are holding spear-throwers in their hands. The condor-heads at the tips of the throwers are to symbolize, perhaps, the flight of the darts. 22.5 × 31 cm. Nazca Valleys (?), S. Peru. Coastal Tiahuanaco culture, about 700 to 900 A. D. The Brooklyn Museum, Brooklyn, No. L 48.13. Lent by Mr. and Mrs. A. Bradley Martin. Courtesy of Mr. and Mrs. A. Bradley Martin and the Brooklyn Museum.

101. Cloak in Gobelin technique: On olive ground-colour weeping jaguar heads change with stepped or winged volutes. Colours: Light-red, dark-red, golden ochre, brown, black, white, obviously in ritual alternation. Size 118 × 110 cm. Nazca-valleys, Southern Peru. Coastal Tiahuanaco culture, about 700 to 900 A. D. H. and M. Gaffron Collection, Chicago.

102. Detail of a cloak in Gobelin technique showing the motive of the 'tiger eyes': extremely simplified jaguar-heads with the 'trail of tears' (pointing downward), teeth consisting of two fangs (adjoining the trail of tears), and nose, indicated by a simple rectangle. Alternating with stepped or winged volutes into which again are inserted tiger eyes. The six panels of the broad middle stripe, from upper left, represent these figures: Jaguar

symbol, upright; jaguar symbol, upside down; volute, wing downward; volute, wing upward; jaguar symbol, upright; jaguar symbol, upside down. Juxtaposed to each of these six figures are – quite narrow, as though compressed like herbarium specimens – their 'complementary' figures, e. g., in the middle (panel 3 and 4), hard to recognize in this reduced and compressed shape, but still retaining *all* of the four iconographically essential elements: tiger eye, trail of tears, fangs, and block nose. The compressed volutes adjoining the jaguar-heads above and below do not exhibit the motive of the eyes. How important completeness was in rendering these hieroglyphical images is revealed by the narrow border stripe at the left side. It contains *all* of the details of the broad stripe in the middle, irrespective of the fact that they are all but unrecognisable; no space was left for them to be placed in the broad middle-panels, but placed they had to be, and that in their entirety; they had to, because on them depended the magical efficacy of this cloak of the dead. There are not many examples to demonstrate the importance of meaning in Old Peruvian imagery as clearly as does this border-stripe at first sight filled with nothing but coloured lines. Length of portion shown 37 cm. Nazca Valleys, S. Peru. Coastal Tiahuanaco culture, about 700 to 900 A. D.

Museum für Völkerkunde, Munich.

103. Portion of a fragmentary cloak in Gobelin technique, with woven condor-heads wearing crowns. The design consists of intricately arranged rectangular crowned condor-heads and stepped or winged volutes. One of the heads shows comparatively distinctly (right upper corner, where the tissue is damaged: below the hole, the eye; to the right of it the bill; to the left of the eye a symbol for the ear; above the eye the crown, with cubes attached to the outer lobes.) Much as the entire structure and lineament of the design, and particularly its soft, dreamlike colours, are capable of enchanting us, it is filled with meaning in every outline; and in so far as the present fragment does make us feel this, it may be taken as one of the finest examples of the sumptuous, hieroglyphic image-textiles of early Tiahuanaco, Nazca, Paracas, and Mochica cultures.

Length of the reproduced portion 58 cm. Material: Warp, cotton, weft, wool. Nazca Valleys, S. Peru.

Coastal Tiahuanaco culture, about 700 to 900 A.D. Museum für Völkerkunde, Munich; presented by H. and M. Gaffron.

104. Cap with four tips in 'simili-velours' technique (cf. K. G. Izikowitz, *L'origine probable de la technique du simili-velours Pérouvien.* Journal de la Société des Américanistes, Paris 1933, pp. 9–16). Four figures; their limbs rendered in cubical forms; symbolical in character, free of realistic tendencies. (A wing, usually found to issue from the back of these 'genii', here springs from the head.) Very bright, brilliant colours.

Breadth: 17 cm. Nazca Valleys, S. Peru. Coastal Tiahuanaco culture, about 700 to 900 A. D. Museum für Völkerkunde, Munich. Formerly Heinrich Hardt Collection.

105. Ceremonial Hat, decorated with heads and rhombuses; mosaic work made of feathers in many colours.

(cp. pl. 102, where jaguar-heads in similar manner are associated with volutes.) Height 17 cm. Nazca Valleys (?), S. Peru. Coastal Tiahuanaco culture, about 700 to 900 A. D.

The Brooklyn Museum, New York. Courtesy of the Museum.

106. Two Chalk-powder Containers. (This powder was – and still is – chewed with coca-leaves, a stimulant enhancing efficiency and abating thirst and hunger.) These two containers are precious works of art, produced for ceremonial purposes (the cult of the dead?), and of a rare beauty.

Top: Smooth and polished snail-shell into which is incrusted the figure of a god in Tiahuanaco style in dark brown wood and shell. The god holds in his hand a trophy-head of fine shell-mosaic The handsome effect of the colours – ivory white of the snail, a warm dark brown in the figure – is not lost in this reproduction. Height 7 cm.

Below: Carved antler(?) with inlay of shell-mosaic in various colours (among which appears a magnificent deep violet) representing a god in Tiahuanaco style. The stopper is surmounted by some sort of helmet in the shape of an animal-head. This head is distinguished by powerfully glancing eyes which again call to mind the Pacheco heads (pls. 109–112). As in the preceding case, we have before our eyes one of the most exquisite works of plastic miniature art of ancient Peru, the best of which proves, as a rule, to be in Tiahuanaco style. Height 10.5 cm. Both pieces from Nazca

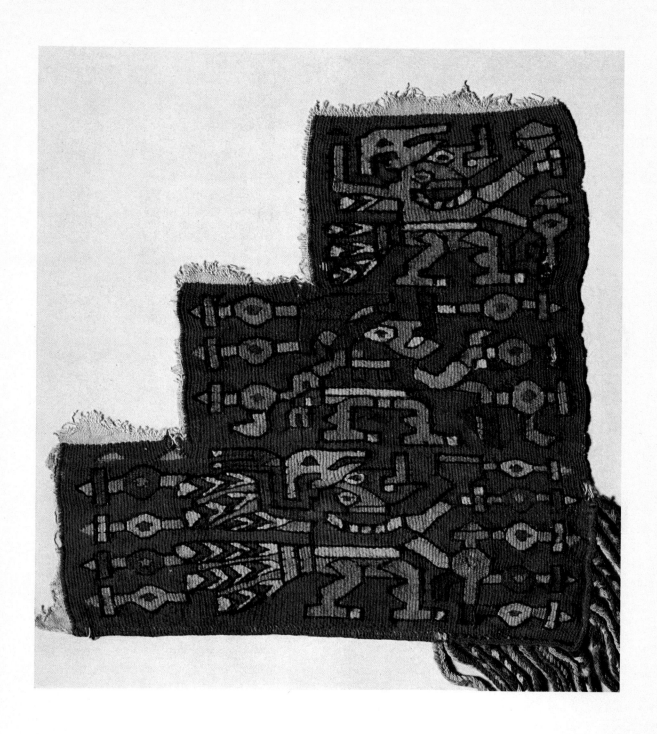

III

Valleys, S. Peru. Coastal Tiahuanaco culture, about 700 to 900 A. D.
Norbert Mayrock Collection.

107. Spear-thrower of dark hardwood with a handle in carved bone. Mythical being, carved in the grand manner of Tiahuanaco, with ghostly eyes in turquoise inlay, resembling the haunting round eyes in the fragment on plate 121. His shoulder is bitten by a dragon bristling with spikes; from his hand is dangling a trophy-head executed as delicately as an ivory miniature. In this weapon for ceremonial but not practical use, suited to some supernatural being's but not men's needs; in the two chalk-containers adorned with secret symbols, shown in the preceding plate, and perhaps also in the woven myths from Paracas, a salient feature in ancient Peruvian art manifests itself: something very like fairy-tales, unreal, averse to any imitative rendering. Length 58.8 cm.; height of carved handle 10.5 cm. The projection for holding the butt of the spear, a small double cone, is of cast copper. The handle is lashed to the stick with fine cords covered by some kind of resin or bitumen. Nazca Valleys, (Palpa area?), S. Peru. Coastal Tiahuanaco culture, about 700 to 900 A. D.
Norbert Mayrock Collection.

108. Top: Ear-plug of dark brown wood incrusted with coloured shell. The head represented, with typical Tiahuanaco style crown over a dotted turban, is strongly reminiscent of the heads from Pacheco (pls. 109–113). Incidentally the head, as it may be noted besides, undeniably resembles that of Queen Teje, also of dark brown wood, in Berlin, Ägyptisches Museum. Length 5,9 cm. Nazca Valleys, S. Peru. Coastal Tiahuanaco culture, about 700 to 900 A. D.
Norbert Mayrock Collection.
Bottom left: Small figure of stone with shell inlays. Height 6.5 cm. Nazca Region? Tiahuanaco culture, about 700–900 A. D.
The Cleveland Museum of Art. In memory of Mr. and Mrs. Henry Humphreys, gift of their daughter, Helen. Courtesy, Cleveland Museum.
Bottom right: Hand carved of shell, inlaid with a chained demon or god in coloured shell turquoise and gold. Height 6.5 cm. Tiahuanaco culture, about 700–900 A. D. Paramonga, N. Peruvian coast. Collection Norbert Mayrock.

109. Fragment of a clay head painted with geometric patterns in white. Height 8.6 cm. Pacheco, Valley of the Rio Grande de Nazca, S. Peru. Coastal Tiahuanaco culture, about 500 to 800 A. D.
H. and M. Gaffron Collection, Chicago.

110. Fragment of a clay head with lacquer-like dark crimson slip. Part of a large urn? (cp. pl. 113.). Height 10 cm. Pacheco, Valley of the Rio Grande de Nazca, S. Peru. Coastal Tiahuanaco culture, about 500 to 800 A. D.
H. and M. Gaffron Collection, Chicago.

111. Fragment of a clay head with lacquer-like dark crimson coating. Height 10 cm. Pacheco, Valley of the Rio Grande de Nazca, S. Peru. Coastal Tiahuanaco culture, about 500 to 800 A. D.
H. and M. Gaffron Collection, Chicago.

112. Top: Small figurine of a mother with a baby in arms. Above his head, on his mother's breast, the tiny white fingernails of the baby can be seen. At the back of the figurine, there is a round orifice which, when blown over gently, produces Aeolian sounds like low cries, sighs or moans. Height 7 cm. From the Nazca Valleys; probably from Pacheco, Valley of the Rio Grande de Nazca (or from Atarco, Taruga Valley?), S. Peru. Coastal Tiahuanaco culture, about 500 to 800 A. D.
Museum für Völkerkunde, Munich.
Bottom: Fragment of a small clay head with face-paint and ornamental discs at the nose. The cap-like cover may be a dance-mask. Found at Pacheco, Valley of the Rio Grande de Nazca, between 1900–1910. (Like the fragments on pls. 109–111, 113, 115). Height 6 cm. Coastal Tiahuanaco culture, about 500 to 800 A. D.
H. and M. Gaffron Collection, Chicago.

113. Fragment of a clay head with lacquer-like dark crimson coating that shows a tendency to flake off. Part of a large urn? Height 16 cm. Thickness of shard at lower edge, 10–13 mm. Pacheco, Valley of the Rio Grande de Nazca, S. Peru. Coastal Tiahuanaco culture, about 500 to 800 A.D. Like the preceding two pieces, this fragment, found together with similar ones, obviously was no funeral gift (cp. H. Ubbelohde-Doering, *Tonplastik aus Nazca*, Ipek, 1927, pp. 67 ff.). When visiting the site in 1932, I found the assumption about local conditions as advanced in that article was correct. The discoverer told me that these shards came to light as shards at a well-worked site under a big old Huarango-tree near Pacheco in the first decade of this century.
H. and M. Gaffron Collection, Chicago.

114. Recumbent white llama with reddish-violet dots; high-fired, sonorous stoneware. The white paint is dull, lacquer-like. Ears, nostrils, mouth, and hooves are brick-red; the eyes, grey with black iris. From the back of the animal rises a cylindrical spout, determining the figure's function as a libation vessel. Around the spout, a Tiahuanaco style ornament in white, yellow, crimson, and black. The left hind leg was broken off when the vessel was deposited in the tomb, as is evident from the fact that the break had been closed before interment by unspun cotton that has turned brown with age. It is indeed possible that the leg was broken on purpose in order to open a way for the 'soul' of the vessel, so that it might serve the dead. There are several instances of pre-Columbian clay vessels with their bottoms perforated to become serviceable to the dead. Height 20 cm., length 17.5 cm. Atarco, Taruga Valley, Nazca region, S. Peru. Coastal Tiahuanaco culture, about 500 to 800 A. D.
Museum für Völkerkunde, Munich.

115. Head of a llama, fragment from a comparatively large clay figure. Height 8 cm. Black in colour, except for lips and ears which are red. Found in this fragmentary state near Pacheco, Valley of the Rio Grande de Nazca between 1900 and 1910. In the twenties, J. C. Tello discovered at the same site fragments of large-sized painted llama-figures. Having been restored since, these figures are among the most beautiful objects now treasured in the Museo Nacional de Arqueología at Lima (Magdalena).
H. and M. Gaffron Collection, Chicago.

116. Clay vessel in the shape of a fish. Body blackish-grey with white dots; handle and spout, dull crimson-red; head white; eyeballs, yellowish with black iris; mouth, red. The fish, no doubt, is a magical symbol of water. Length 19 cm. From a coastal Tiahuanaco shaft-tomb. Locarí, Valley of Huayurí, Nazca region, S. Peru. About 500 to 800 A. D. Museum für Völkerkunde, Munich.

117. Sacrificial vessel of grey unpainted clay in the shape of a llama. Legs and tail broken off. On the whole of similar build to the jaguar vessel on plate 118. Height 18,5 cm., length 27 cm. Ruins of Tiahuanaco. Tiahuanaco culture at Titicaca Lake, about 500 A. D. or earlier.
Museum für Völkerkunde, Munich.

118. Libation vessel, shaped as a roaring jaguar. Body red-brown; head and collar dark grey (in remnants);

tail black. The shield-like collar is characteristic of these Tiahuanaco style vessels in the shape of jaguars or condors from the Titicaca Highland area. Libations were poured through the mouth of the animal. Height 17,7 cm. Ruins of Tiahuanaco, close to the south eastern tip of Titicaca Lake, 3800 m. above sea-level. From the classical stage of the Tiahuanaco culture, about 500 to 700 A. D. Museum für Völkerkunde, Munich.

119. Clay fragment: human head with remnants of a red-brown slip. Height 8 cm. Ruins of Tiahuanaco. Tiahuanaco culture at Titicaca Lake, about 500 to 800 A. D.
Museum für Völkerkunde, Munich.

120. Reddish brown clay fragment of a small human head with a very expressive mouth: 'the living' (as the preceding fragment) facing 'the dead' on the following plate. From the Calasasaya Stone Pillar Quadrangle in the Tiahuanaco Ruins. Tiahuanaco culture at Titicaca Lake, about 500 to 700 A. D.
Photograph enlarged; original size 3 × 4,8 cm.
Private Collection.

121. Fragment of grey clay, 6,8 cm. high, with incised outlines that represent the dead man as though conceived in his new superhuman existence as a demon, demigod, or deity. On the other side (of this book as well as of existence), the living, amazingly animated even in the fragment; here, the other world as imagined by the Ancient Peruvians. Ruins of Tiahuanaco at Titicaca Lake. Tiahuanaco culture in the Southern Highland, about 500 to 800 A. D.
Museum für Völkerkunde, Munich.

122. Top: So-called Sun Gate of Tiahuanaco, Bolivian Highland. Made of one huge slab of volcanic rock (andesite), decorated with a frieze in relief: towards a personage in the centre who stands erect on some sort of throne and overtops them, genii proceed in superposed rows. On both sides the outermost three figures in each row were left unfinished. Below this frieze heads with aureoles encircled by meandering bands. (See also pl. 123.). Height of the gate: 3 m., width 3,82 m., depth 0,42–0,48 m., weight about 9500 kg. Tiahuanaco culture, about 700 to 800 A. D. (?)
Bottom: Large monolithic statue, discovered in 1932 by Wendell C. Bennet, in the small temple east of the 'Calasasaya' Stone Pillar Quadrangle at Tiahuanaco, and now erected at La Paz. Length 7,30 m., length of head 1,90 m. Red sand-

stone. (Photo taken shortly after the discovery in 1932). Tiahuanaco culture, about 700 to 800 A. D. (?)

123. Top: Running genii on the right side of the gate; at the right edge, the unfinished figures. Bottom: Lower frieze in the relief of the Sun Gate; portion above the passage.

124. Sun Gate at Tiahuanaco, viewed from left corner to demonstrate the wall-rug character of the relief and the powerful relief of the central figure that rises above the swarm of the genii.

125. Side view of the Sun Gate, showing relief of the central figure.

126. Painting on a fragmentary goblet from Tiahuanaco: fabulous animal with the head and wings of a condor, the body of a quadruped, and human feet. Tiahuanaco culture, about 500 to 800 A. D.
Height 11 cm.
Museum für Völkerkunde, Munich.

127. Clay painted beaker from Tiahuanaco. Below, jaguar demon bearing magical symbols; middle zone, a frieze of human heads with turbans dotted white; above, strongly stylized human heads, representations of demons or deities. Tiahuanaco culture, about 500 to 800 A. D.
Height 18 cm.
Museum für Völkerkunde, Munich.

128. Fragments of clay vessels with painted and incised figures of jaguars or pumas, the heads of which are rendered plastically. Height, upper fragment 8.5 cm, lower fragment 13 cm. Pucara, Highland South West of Titicaca Lake.
Museum für Völkerkunde, Munich.

129. Carved posts (roof-supports) of very hard Huarango wood, with heads and figures of spirits of the dead (ancestors?) with pan-pipes. Height of the posts at the left: 178 and 176 cm., post at the right 168 cm. Nazca Valleys. From the coastal Tiahuanaco culture or a related sphere – about 500 to 800 A. D.; possibly older.
Museum für Völkerkunde, Munich.

130. Large ruby-red veil. So-called net-warp technique: each panel has its special warp and weft, so that the whole is composed of numerous small weavings. At the left, demons rising; at the right, demons descending. Topmost, six single symbols, of which the first, the third, the fourth and the sixth are stylised trophy-heads. These heads, which had a magical significance for fertility of the fields, are also seen at the hands and feet of

the demons. Colours: yellow, brown, red, and blue. Material: wool. Length 1.90 m., width 97 cm. Nazca region, S. Peru. 'Epigonal Culture' (Uhle), succeeding the Nazca culture and partly corresponding to Kroeber's 'Nazca Y'. On the basis of excavations I made in 1932, I call this culture the 'Morro Culture' because the tombs yielding this kind of fabric are situated chiefly on the 'morros' (hills bordering the valleys), and because the term 'Epigonal' involves a deprecation that is not really justified. About 400 to 600 A. D.
Museum für Völkerkunde, Munich; Heinrich Hardt Collection.

131. Large bluish-black veil with red ornament, tie-dyed ('Plangi' technique; cp. pl. 83 above). Ornaments forming chains and meanders. Wool. Width 90 cm. From the Southern Nazca Valleys, S. Peru. Between 500 and 1000 A. D.
Museum für Völkerkunde, Munich.

132. Tapestry with a design of numerous strongly stylised animal figures (most easily recognised are birds in the middle zone), trophy-heads (similar to those in the fabric on pl. 130), trophy-heads with bristly hair (lowermost right and left), and 'geometrical' ornaments of symbolic meaning. One of the Old Peruvian fabrics, demonstrating impressively and convincingly their pictographical character. Colours: Red, yellow, blue, black. Material: Weft woollen, warp cotton. Size 184 × 235 cm. Nazca region (Valley of Rio Santa Cruz or of Rio Grande?). S. Peru.
Like the fabric on pl. 130, a later echo of Old-Nazca of the South – with new features added that came from the Andean regions. About 500 to 800 A. D.
Museum für Völkerkunde, Munich.

133. Tapestry with broad tassels. The figures represented are entirely imaginary, free from realistic tendencies: significance is everything; natural forms, nothing. Length 120 cm., width 90 cm. Possibly from the Southernmost valley – Las Trancas – of the Nazca region, whence two or three fabrics with similarly large configurations have come. Styles of several cultures unite in the design: conventionalized residues of the art of Old Nazca (in the interior of the two main figures); forms akin to those of Early Mochica in the North (in the globular heads at the left border); features from Chavín (in the snakes with their polychrome scales which issue from and turn back to the

main figures); finally, an element of still unknown origin, asserting itself in various details as well as in the entire composition; perhaps, but not necessarily, derived from the mountain region in the south. Between 500 and 800 A. D.
The Brooklyn Museum, Brooklyn; courtesy of the Museum.

134. Clay vessel with porcelain-white surface, on which is painted in bright colours the figure of a deity floating in the air. In his one hand, he holds two trophy-heads; in the other (near the left margin), a club-like stick. The yellow discs to the right and left appear to represent golden ornamental discs. Colours: crimson, light red, yellow, grey, white, and black. Height 14.3 cm. Tunga, Valley of the Rio de las Trancas, Nazca region. The vessel is extraordinarily light: a property which, according to the collector, Dr. E. Gaffron, is characteristic of the ceramics from the Tunga area. Comparably light ware occurs, to the writer's knowledge, only at Nievería and, in the trophy-head on pl. 161, Paracas Cavernas. The bulk of the ceramics of Paracas Cavernas shows however a thick and soft body of much heavier weight (cp. pls. 160, 239). Among the treasure-hunters, Tunga (besides Cahuachi) is known as the site yielding the finest Nazca wares. Nazca culture, about 300 to 600 A. D.
H. and M. Gaffron Collection, Chicago.

135. Top: Clay bowl, painted in white slip. Frieze of colibris between flowering branches: the colibri, appearing in Spring, was considered a little deity of Spring. Colours: the colibri in red, white, grey, and black; the branches in dark red, with black outlines. Interior of the bowl: dark crimson-red. Height 9.5 cm. Nazca Valleys, Nazca culture, about 300 to 600 A. D.
Museum für Völkerkunde, Munich.
Bottom: Thinly potted bowl decorated with the image of an anthropomorphic god, painted on white ground. He wears a mask of feline features, and from his back emanates a train occupied by trophy-heads and arrows pointing downward. Diam. 13.5 cm.
Nazca region, Valley of the Rio Grande, Chillo area, Nazca culture, about 300 to 600 A. D.
Museum für Völkerkunde, Munich.

136. Clay bottle with mythological representations painted on white ground. In the upper picture, the rain-god, who wears a fruit-crown and from whose mouth gush forth two streams of water,

represented pictographically by crested snakes filled with tadpoles. In the lower picture, showing the opposite side of the bottle, the god's assistants are depicted, the rain-lads, as they scoop water from the large rain-urn into tumblers (of a type scarcely met with in Nazca tombs) which they carry away to where it shall rain. Rain-lads assisting the raingod were known also in Old Mexico (cf. W. Krickeberg, *Märchen der Azteken und Inkaperuaner, Maya und Muiska*, Jena 1928, p. 34 – after Cod. Mex. Pint., p. 230, where there is given a description which could not be illustrated more faithfully than by our Nazca painting), and to-day still are, among the Pipil Salvadors (L. Schultze Jena, *Indiana* II, Jena 1935, p. 18 ff.; cf. also H. U.-Doering, *Altperuanische Gefäßmalereien*, Teil II, Marburg 1931, p. 11 ff. and pl. III). Colours of the rain-god: brick-red, crimson-red, yellow, grey, white, and black. Height 16.8 cm. Nazca Valleys (Tunga?). Nazca culture, about 300 to 600 A. D.
Museum für Völkerkunde, Munich.

137. Clay bottle, painted. On white ground, plants with fruit or flowers. Colours: black, soft violet, and a lacquer-like dark crimson at the spouts and the handle. Height 16,7 cm. Nazca Valleys, S. Peru. Nazca culture, about 300 to 600 A. D.
H. and M. Gaffron Collection, Chicago.

138. Large clay bowl decorated in the interior with fishes. Diameter 30 cm. Huayurí, Valley of the Rio Santa Cruz, Nazca region. Nazca culture, about 300 to 600 A. D.
Museum für Völkerkunde, Munich.

139. Clay bottle in the shape of a frog, symbol of humidity and water. The feet are painted in black on the white belly. At the back, stripes. Nazca Valleys, S. Peru. Nazca culture, about 300 to 600 A. D. Museum für Völkerkunde, Munich.

140. Head of the spirit of the dead, shaped as a tumbler. In Ancient Nazca paintings, eyes such as these, with the iris half covered, signify the eyes of the dead or of spirits of the dead. Spirit-nature and transfiguration into a new form of existence are expressed by the broad painting round the eyes, by which birds' eyes are indicated: the dead becomes a bird-demon.
Colours: face, dull greyish-yellow; paint around the eyes, black; mouth, white; the 'turban' in stripes alternately white and red. Height 17 cm. Nazca Valleys, S. Peru. Nazca culture, about 300 to 600 A. D. H. and M. Gaffron Collection, Chicago.

141. Left: Clay bottle with polychrome paint on black
ground. Figure of a leaping demon composed of
head, arms, and legs. Upon his own head he
carries a tower of heads, and with his hands he
grasps bands with volute-like excrescences. In
regard to his towering crown with its bristling
volute-ends, the demon resembles the famous
image of a deity on the so-called Raimondi-Mono-
lith, a stone-relief from Chavín de Huantar
(cp. text-figure p. 37); he resembles the central
figure of the Sun Gate at Tiahuanaco only in that
he carries some sort of ceremonial symbols in his
raised hands. Height 18.8 cm. Nazca Valleys,
S. Peru. Nazca culture, about 300 to 600 A. D.
Museum für Völkerkunde, Munich.

Right: Clay goblet with painted decor arranged
in four zones. Lowermost zone: yellow discs with
central red dots on black ground. Second zone:
Procession of small birds in black and white,
dotted white and black, respectively, on brick-
red ground. The discs again appear in the third
zone. Topmost, a broad frieze in brick-red with
two dancers carrying feather-staffs (with white
feathers) in their right hands (at the left margin)
and clubs in their left hands; small arrows shoot
(blow-pipe arrows?) and strange white balls hover
around them. The dancer's face is yellow; his
arms and legs are red; the fillet grey with white
feathers. He wears a white shirt, and grey and
yellow garments. – We know nothing about the
meaning of these dancers; nor, to the writer's
knowledge, have such staffs been found in tombs,
but small sticks (of about half a metre's length)
with gay coloured feathers have been found.
Height 20.5 cm. Nazca Valleys, S. Peru. Late
Nazca culture, about 500 to 600 A. D.
H. and M. Gaffron Collection, Chicago.

142. Ceremonial cloak, richly adorned with figures in
four panels: first and third from left, white
rhombi with geometrical ornaments; second and
fourth, processions of warriors. In these two
panels we see on the left rows of warriors with
rich head-dress marching toward left (downward)
and glancing from their eyes of the dead; at the
right, marching toward right (upward), rows of
uncrowned figures with eyes of the living. They
stand on a ruby-red ground and are in white,
yellow, blue, and violet. The border of tassels in
dark golden yellow. Originally, the outlines of the
warriors were black. This black which apparently
had contained humic acid has destroyed the dyed

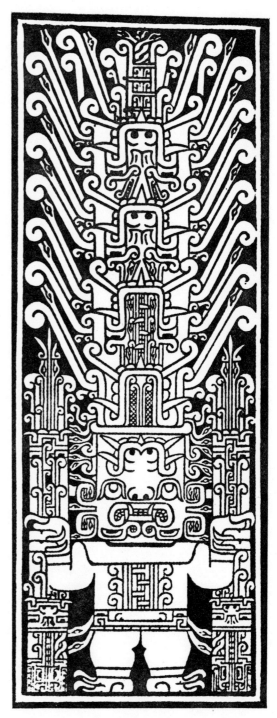

Relief on the so-called Raimondi monolith,
Chavín de Huantar

threads. As a consequence, the fabric looks as
though it was woven with slits; in the present
reproduction, a piece of dark cloth laid under the

fabric makes the figures appear more distinctly. In the middle of the upper margin, there is the slit for the head to pass through. At the upper corners, short projections form tasselled sleeves. The decoration is identical on both sides. Height 75 cm, width 115 cm. Material: woollen weft. Nazca Valleys, S. Peru. Late (?) Nazca culture, about 400 to 600 A. D.

Museum für Völkerkunde, Munich; Heinrich Hardt Collection.

143. Large bluish-black veil, in *à-jour* technique. Decorated with fish-like demons of the sea, alternately pointing upward and downward. In the border, numerous small birds between flowers and fruits in three-dimensional needlework. The design of the veil symbolizes the ceaselessly billowing sea, sum of the waters that bring fertility; the birds, flowers and fruits mean Spring, vegetable growth, fruit-bearing plantations. Placed in the hands of the dead, these images were thought to produce magically all the effects expressed in them and thus fulfil the wishes of those who wove them and put them in the graves. Nazca culture, S. Peru. (Needlework in the round as in the present border is typical of this early culture.) About 300 to 600 A. D.

The border is in part destroyed. It did not originally run through but embraced the shorter edges only to the extent still seen in the reproduction; the greater part of these edges was left unframed. In this the arrangement resembles the large embroidered fabrics from Paracas (Necropolis; cp. pls. 148–152). The fabric in the present plate appears to be designed as a magical space open at the narrow sides: in these directions the sea-demons move – not toward the long borders, which like garlands of flowers close the magical space of the veil against the outer world. Length 142 cm., width 135 cm. Material: wool. Cahuachi, Valley of the Rio Grande de Nazca, S. Peru.

Museum für Völkerkunde, Munich.

144. Painted cotton fabric of simple texture with gay coloured woollen border in needlework typical of the Nazca culture. The painting symbolizes abundant crops; showing the produce endangered by birds, it possibly also means that the birds shall be kept away by its magic power. The border may also have its significance. Length 87 cm, breadth 60 cm. Nazca culture, about 300 to 600 A. D. Nazca Valleys, S. Peru.

Museum für Völkerkunde, Munich; Heinrich Hardt Collection.

145. Top: Lilac coloured cotton shirt with starlike flowers, or floriform stars painted in dark blue. Length 57 cm., width 126 cm. Paracas, S. Peru. Paracas Necropolis culture, between 200 and 600 A. D.

Museum für Völkerkunde, Munich.

Norbert Mayrock Collection.

I know of fragments of similarly painted, violet veil fabrics coming from the lower valley of the Rio Grande de Nazca.

Bottom: Border fragment of a ruby-red fabric in meshwork from Paracas, S. Peru. Animal demons of varying sizes form an intricately locked pattern. The decor is characteristic of the borders of the Paracas Necropolis culture, between 200 and 600 A. D. Size of portion shown 40 cm. Material: wool.

Norbert Mayrock Collection.

146. Border in knot-work, with threads diagonally arranged like crossing zigzag lines running from edge to edge. Width 10 cm. Material wool. Paracas.

Museum für Völkerkunde, Munich. Heinrich Hardt Collection.

(cp. R. d'Harcourt, *Les Textiles anciens du Pérou*, Paris 1934, p. 78, text, fig. 47, and plate LVI, 3).

147. Detail of a border in meshwork. Figure of a warrior with ceremonial face-paint, holding a trophy-head in his hands. Smaller trophy-heads adorn his garment at the breast and the hem. Width of portion shown 14 cm. Material: wool. Paracas Necropolis culture. Between 200 and 600 A. D. Paracas, S. Peru.

Museum für Völkerkunde, Munich; Heinrich Hardt Collection.

148. Large fabric (Manto) from Paracas, S. Peru. The dark central field, which at the sides is open, is embroidered in regular chequer-order with figures of condors spreading their wings. In the border, meshwork-stitched condors in pairs. This and the series of shrouds presented in pls. 151, 152, 154, 155 are among the most exquisite textiles from Paracas. Material: embroidery in the central field and meshwork in the border are woollen. Paracas Necropolis culture. Between 200 and 600 A. D.

The Brooklyn Museum, Brooklyn; Courtesy Brooklyn Museum.

149. Middle part of the preceding Manto.

150. Single condor figure from the central field of the Manto in pl. 148.

151. Large fabric from Paracas, S. Peru. The dark central field with its characteristic openings at the narrow sides is filled with fishes in pairs arranged chequer-wise. The same design recurs in meshwork in the border, where however a tiny fish is added to and encircled by each pair of the large fishes. Material: dark field with embroideries; meshwork of the border, wool. Paracas Necropolis culture. Between 200 and 600 A.D. The Brooklyn Museum, Brooklyn. Courtesy Brooklyn Museum.

152. Detail of the preceding Manto.

153. Shoulder-cape from Paracas, S. Peru, with sumptuous *décor* in meshwork (cp. pl. 151, 152) and long multi-coloured tassels to cover the shoulders. Material: wool. Paracas Necropolis culture, between 200 and 600 A.D. The Brooklyn Museum, Brooklyn, Courtesy Brooklyn Museum.

154. One half of a large fabric (Manto) from Paracas, S. Peru. The dark central field is embroidered with double-headed birds of prey ('double-eagles'), which hold snakes in their claws and, in columns of alternating direction, form a chessboard pattern. The birds recur enlarged in meshwork in the broad pattern. The eyes of these birds are characterized by three downward stripes, comparable to the eyes of the death-spirits in Nazca vase paintings (pl. 140). (According to E. Yakovleff, these stripes are a mark of the falcon; Revista del Museo Nacional, Lima, 1932, No. 1, p. 50 f.). Length 145 cm., width 125 cm. Material: main fabric and embroidery in wool; meshes of the border, wool. Paracas Necropolis culture. Between 200 and 600 A.D. Museum für Völkerkunde, Munich. Presented by Heinrich Hardt.

155. Large fabric (Manto) from Paracas, S. Peru. Variant form of the Manto, with transverse stripes crossing the dark central field in meshwork, the technique used in the border. The same figures appear in both stripes and border: animals and interlocked serrated bands. Prevalent colour: ruby-red. An 'opening' of the narrow sides is achieved here by way of omission of the tassels in front of the 'gates', while the border itself runs through but is reduced in width by almost one half at the narrow sides of the fabric. The meaning of the arrangement seemingly differs from that in the chessboard-Mantos of the preceding plates.

Material: dark ground, wool; border meshes and transverse stripes, wool. Paracas Necropolis culture. Between 200 and 600 A.D. Museum für Völkerkunde, Frankfurt am Main; formerly Dr. Arndt Collection.

156. Mesh-work strip, Paracas Necropolis culture (between 200 and 600 A.D.). Descending (ape ?-) demon carrying a broad, entirely nascoid crown, with polychrome bands waving upward and consisting of joined symbols ending in two heads. These hold in their teeth figures which are nothing else than abbreviated renderings of the crown of the (ape ?-) demon. From its mouth emanates a broad band becoming an animal with hands and feet; its one hand seizes the hair of a large trophy-head. The short-armed demon holds in its left hand a fan and in its right a staff as well as in each of its ape-shaped prehensile toes (above) an abbreviated trophy head.

The whole design, made in needlework, is either a rendering of Nazca vase paintings, or, these Nazca paintings are copies of woven designs of the Paracas Necropolis culture. One is, however, inclined to assume that such intricate and complex designs in textiles have been, in simplified form, reproduced on vases, rather than that the more simple vase paintings of the Nazca, in copying needlework, developed into the much more intricate woven designs of the Paracas Necropolis textiles. If this is true, the Nazca potters should be regarded as later copyist. At any rate, these potters were still coexistent with the weavers of the Paracas Necropolis, and both arts must once have been coeval. However, not all Nazca designs and figures are akin to the woven Paracas myths. It would be an important task precisely to determine in the Nazca designs all the figures corresponding to those in the Paracas Necropolis textiles thus isolating this element of Nazca art. It would be very interesting to see what then would remain. (Regarding this question of priority cp. also E. Yakovleff y *I. C. Muelle, Un fardo funerario de Paracas;* Revista del Museo Nacional, tomo III, Lima 1934, pp. 148–150. Both writers ascribe the priority to the Nazca paintings). Length of strip shown 21 cm. Material: wool. Paracas, S. Peru. Norbert Mayrock Collection.

157. Part of a mesh-work strip in a Manto from Paracas, S. Peru; cp. pl. 155. Serrated bands, the

ends of which are interlocked in angular spirals; between them, smaller and larger quadrupeds; in the lower corners, millepede-like creatures. Width of the ornamented strip 13.5 cm. Material: wool. Paracas Necropolis culture. Between 200 and 600 A. D.
Norbert Mayrock Collection.

158–159. Large blanket in three-dimensional needlework and openwork from Paracas, S. Peru (comparable to the veil in pl. 143). In the quadrangular fields thirty-two figures of demons in the shape of men, birds, butterflies (?), frogs and lobsters, framed as shown in plate 159: as though caught in the square nets to conjure water and fertility. The border is teeming with small manlike fertility demons, figures resembling fish, and realistically rendered birds and plants (like the border figures in pl. 143): a magical compendium which – although perhaps we never shall be able fully to interpret its secrets – in the most telling way illustrates the magic worked into textiles. The blanket was found lying folded on the breast of the dead. Length 102 cm., width 51.5 cm. Material: wool. Colours: crimson, pinkish, blue, green, brown, yellow.
Paracas Necropolis culture, between 200 and 600 A. D.
Göteborg Museum, Göteborg. (cp. also R. d'Harcourt, *Un tapis brodé de Paracas*, Journal de la Société des Américanistes, N. S. t. XXXVII, 1948, pp. 241–257).

160. Clay bowl. Outlines of the ornament incised; colours thickly applied after firing: dark yellow and crimson red on black ground (partly fallen off; at the right, frame and rings are preserved). Rectangularly stylized head of a demon or a deity with teeth of a beast of prey; the teeth and the incision are reminiscent of Chavín (cp. pl. 235), while the rectangularity of form compares with Tiahuanaco. Diameter 16.5 cm. Ocucaje, Ica Valley, S. Peru. Paracas Cavernas culture, between ± 0 and 500 A. D.
Museum für Völkerkunde, Munich.

161. Clay bottle in the shape of a trophy-head. Exceedingly thinly potted (1–2 mm. in the middle parts) and light as a feather (weight 270 g.). Incised contours; colours applied after firing, apparently coagulated at several spots. Against the dark yellow of the face, the cherry-red of the lips and the zigzags thence emanating appear like lacquer: a colour substance I observed nowhere else in Peruvian pottery. The teeth bared, dazzling white between the lacquer red of the lips. The hair olive-green, with a red band laid on it. The two slender spouts, one of which is closed and functions as a whistle, and the broad bridging handle between them, are in a dark red hue. Conspicuous is the modelling of the forehead: obviously in accordance with customary artificial deformation. This rigid head in the soft sheen of its unreal colouring, lying like Mimir's head before the onlooker, is not only one of the most extraordinary specimens of the Paracas Cavernas culture, to which it belongs, but one of the masterpieces of Ancient Peruvian art generally. The conjuring power in this face will be felt even to-day. This power springs not only from the artist's eminent faculties; it likewise depends on the strong magical tension of this head, its forms, its colours. In Ancient Peru, notably in the early cultures, trophy-heads were considered a magical source of strength, of blessing, of abundant crops. Height 19 cm. Paracas, S. Peru. Paracas Cavernas culture, between ± 0 and 500 A. D.
Norbert Mayrock Collection.
(Recently, a very similar specimen has been acquired by the Göteborg Museum, 35.52.178. It differs in several details from our piece. The zigzag bands are narrower and more acutely pointed; the teeth number eighteen instead of twenty-four; the hair is rendered more schematically; the spouts are slimmer and, lacking the hourglass-like waist, look more conventionalized. (Cf. Henry Wassén, *Tre Föremål från Paracas*, Peru. Särtryck ur Göteborgs Musei Årstryck 1949 och 1950, p. 215).

162. One-eyed 'beggar': clay bottle in the shape of a man offering a sacrifice. His body in a warm dark ochre tone; the sash he wears, alternating in white, crimson, grey, crimson; on his arms, black (tattoo?) ornaments. An example of the art of Nievería which to us may seem a genre-art occasionally verging on the burlesque, something very unlikely to have been in those ancient potters' minds. Height 16.5 cm. Nievería, Central Peruvian coast, near Lima. About 8th to 11th centuries A. D.
H. and M. Gaffron Collection, Chicago.

163. Top: Pottery fragment: pair of birds with a spout between them. Whitish fayence-like body. The forms, in particular the flat wings, are reminiscent of metal work or wood-carvings. Good

example of the peculiar so-called Recuay Pottery (after one of the chief sites in the Upper Santa Valley, N. Peru). About 6th to 9th centuries A. D. Height 16 cm.
Museum für Völkerkunde, Berlin.
Bottom: Clay pot with lug-handle, decorated with stylized animal figures in negative paint. Recuay, Santa Valley, N. Peru. About 6th to 9th centuries A. D. Length 27 cm.
Museum für Völkerkunde, Berlin.

164. Clay bottle shaped as a squatting warrior carrying shield and club. Painted with jagged snakes reminiscent of Nazca styles. Colours: white ground; red (face, etc.), and black. Recuay, Santa Valley, N. Peru. About 6th to 9th centuries A. D. Height 22.2 cm.
Museum für Völkerkunde, Berlin.

165. Left: Panpipe player (?) leading a llama (?). Clay, whitish surface, painted in black and red. Height 20.1 cm.
Right: Small stylized jaguar figure with exaggeratedly broad jaws contrasting with the gracefully set feet and wearing some sort of crown. Height 24 cm.
Both pieces from Recuay, Santa Valley, N. Peru. About 6th to 9th centuries A. D.
Museum für Völkerkunde, Berlin.

166. Terrace steps of the Huaca del Sol, showing erosion through (rare) rainfalls. At the right, the towering pyramid.

167. So-called Huaca del Sol, sanctuary of the sun, near Moche, North Peruvian Coast. Long terrace in steps upon which rises a step-pyramid: largest Old Peruvian architecture at the coast. Built in brick masonry, probably on top of a natural elevation. Total height 41 m., length of the terrace 228 m.
As it presents itself to the onlooker, the building may go back toward the end of the first millenium A. D., that is, between Mochica and Chimú cultures. It is very likely, however, that the building embraces an earlier, much smaller one from the Mochica period (cp. my article: Studien zur Baukunst der nord-peruanischen Küste, to appear in the Baessler Archiv).

168. Mochica reliefs in the interior of the pyramid called 'El Brujo', ('The sorcerer'), north of the Chicama River, at the sea-shore. In the cavities of the reliefs, traces of white, yellow, red, and bluish-grey colour. Here, too, an earlier Mochica pyramid of small dimensions was built over later.

(Cp. my article referred to above, pl. 167, and my book 'Auf den Königsstraßen der Inka', Berlin 1941, p. 49, pl. 325).

169. Vase, 'Florero', with dark brown paint on a yellowish-white ground: dead warrior transfigured into a bird demon with shield and club. Identical figure on the opposite side. Height 30 cm. Huaca de la Campana, near Pampa de Jaguey, Upper Chicama Valley, N. Peru. Mochica culture, about 400 to 600 A. D.
Private Collection.

170-171. Vase paintings in warm dark brown on ivory-white ground: reception of a military commander (or king?) with attendants, pan-pipe blowing priests and musicians playing some instrument like a peal of bells. The armour of the lord (upper figure) consists of rectangular copper plates sewed on the garment. These paintings are among the finest left by the highly artistic Mochica people. Diameter 13.5 cm. Huaca de la Campana, Pampa de Yaguey, N. Peru. Mochica culture, between 400 and 600 A. D.
Museo Nacional de Arqueología, Lima.

172-173. Clay bottle, painted in black-brown and red-brown on ivory-white ground: Ceremonial plucking of leaves or fruit by a demon or deity or a figure wearing a ritual mask. At his back hangs a symbol of unknown significance; at his arm a bag. To the right, a mountainous landscape; to the left (see pl. 172), a kind of platform with two baskets (?), and a disc or bale painted with dots and lines strikingly resembling Maya numeral signs (a formal similarity which must not be considered as a proof of relationship). On top of these three objects, there is a horizontal basketry (?) bench upon which is placed an animal-headed idol (?); it seems as though the plucker is about to proceed devoutly toward this idol. Lowermost, three cacti. Height 24 cm. Huaca de la Campana, Pampa de Yaguey, Chicama Valley, N. Peru.
Mochica culture, about 400 to 600 A. D.
Private Collection.

174-175. Clay vessel with dark brown paintings on ivory-white ground: Fierce combats between differently clad and armed warriors. The victorious, more sumptuously dressed warriors drag the succumbing ones by their hair (their helmets apparently being lost). The victors carry round shields, whereas their opponents have rectangular ones which they wave to no avail. Excellently drawn is the figure of the succumbing man on pl. 175, whose legs are covered by fine incised tattoo patterns. Armament differs in that the defeated group, in addition to club and shield, as carried also by the victors, have lances with barbed heads (pl. 174 left). Round the margin of the convex roof, a frieze of creeping jaguars. Chicama region, N. Peru.

Height 18 cm. Mochica culture, between 400 and 600 A. D.

Norbert Mayrock Collection.

176. Clay bottle with creamy white surface and chocolate-coloured painting: dancing deity – like a dancing Shiva – who assumes the appearance of a crab. The supernatural, daemonic properties of the dancer are symbolized by the rhombic shape of his mouth with two fangs in it, rendered in abbreviated manner. Identical figure on the opposite side of the vessel; between them (under the handle) two sea-demons. Height 26 cm. Mochica culture, N. Peru. Between 400 and 600 A. D.

Museum für Völkerkunde, Munich.

177. Deep, goblet-like clay bowl with crenelated rim. The crenels possibly are symbols of clouds. Inner surface below the rim decorated with the image of an ancient deity, repeated many times in three superposed zones. Lower part left plain. At the outer surface, a frieze of large discs; below these, a design resembling a net. The foot is hollow and is filled with clay pellets or small pebbles which produce rattle-sounds as the goblet is shaken. Height 18.7 cm. Chicama Valley (?), N. Peru. Mochica culture, between 400 and 600 A. D.

H. and M. Gaffron Collection, Chicago.

178. Clay bottle, painted in dark Indian red on white ground and adorned by little frogs in the round: water scenery with fish, aquatic birds and flowers of an aquatic plant (according to Weberbauer). The two frogs, as if emerging from the picture, look up to a third frog which, sitting on top of the spout as though it were on a cliff, looks skyward. Through a complex of symbols, treated fairly realistically, blessing-bringing water is represented to conjure fertility. The neck and the lower part of the belly of the bottle are painted in Indian red. Height 26 cm. Chicama Valley (?), N. Peru. Mochica culture, between 400 and 600 A. D.

H. and M. Gaffron Collection, Chicago.

179. Head of a jaguar (?), fragment of a clay vessel with cream-white surface and paint in Indian red.

Height 11.4 cm. N. Peru. Mochica culture, between 400 and 600 A. D.

H. and M. Gaffron Collection, Chicago.

180–181. Clay bottle painted with battle-scenes. Surmounted by a most extraordinary full-round figure of an eagle or falcon which, armed with shield and club and gigantic in scale, glides like Fate over the painted, ferociously warring world. The bird represents either a dead warrior transfigured into an eagle or falcon, or is the manifestation of a god who intervenes in man's struggles. Height 22 cm. Chicama Valley, N. Peru. Mochica culture, between 400 and 600 A. D.

Private Collection.

182. Clay bottle, painted: nocturnal dance of the dead. Radiating stars show that this takes place at night. The dancers blow pan-pipes and wear dark hoods and capes. Their heads reveal them as dead. At the left, there are large pitchers to hold Chicha (maize beer). If this interpretation is correct, the intoxicating drink is connected with the worship of the dead, as a means to transport the living and delight the dead who dance when night falls.

"For them the sun shines ever in full might
Throughout our earthly night; . . .
And there they take their pleasure as they will,...
with harp or lute:
And blissful where they dwell, beside them still
Dwells at full bloom perfect felicity."

(Pindar, Thrênos, Life after Death. Trsl. by Walter Headlam in: The Oxford Book of Greek Verse in Translation, Oxford 1938.)

Above the pitchers, the dancers, and the stars, a drummer rises like a giant ghost, and with wide open eyes gazes out in the night. We might imagine to hear the hollow rumbling of his drum. That our description does not exhaust the meaning of this most fascinating work is apparent, for instance, from the S-curves at the drummer's sleeves; comparative studies make it likely that these S-curves are lightning symbols. Height 25.5 cm. (without handle). N. Peru. Mochica culture, between 400 and 600 A. D.

Museum für Völkerkunde, Berlin.

183. Pottery twin bottles, connected above and below by a handle and a tube, respectively. The rear bottle is to be filled with water, or some potion

used in sacrifices, to some level above the connecting tube. In the head in front, a small whistle of clay is hidden. If the vessel is so moved that the liquid in the rear vase enters through the connecting tube into the front vase, the air compressed in the latter escapes through the whistle, and through the open mouth of the mask strange sounds like tormented sighs and groans are emitted. Undoubtedly, this kind of vessel (called 'Chifladores' or 'Silvadores', 'whistlers') were not toys, as formerly they were supposed to be, but one of the many forms wherein the all-pervading magic of Ancient Peruvian art became manifest. Height of front bottle ca. 15 cm. Chicama Valley, N. Peru. Mochica culture, between 400 and 600 A. D.
Private Collection.

184. Warrior, about to fasten his head-dress, sitting with crossed legs on top of a clay bottle with white surface. Though warrior, he probably has to do with some ritual ceremony rather than warfare, as is suggested by the large disc adorned with an animal head which towers above his head, a disc representing perhaps some chased gold emblem, part of a ceremonial costume. The disc recurs with the painted runners below. These runners race over sandy hills, and in their hands they carry what appear to be small bags with tips pointing upward (which according to Rafael Larco contain hieroglyphically engraved beans). Worthy of note is the colibri shooting down between the first and second runners. In the sculptures above, head, belly, and limbs are painted India red; so is the painting below. Height 27 cm. Chicama Valley, N. Peru. Mochica culture, between 400 and 600 A. D.
Private Collection.

185. Clay bottle in the shape of a sitting warrior with incised ornamentation on his face (tattooing?) and on his breast (pattern of garment). The eyes possibly had held some inlay. Sand-coloured surface, of a texture partly as smooth as stone. Height 24 cm. Chicama Valley, N. Peru. Early (?) Mochica culture, about 400 A. D. (?)
Private Collection.

186. Clay bottle in the shape of a squatting figure with wrinkled face. The body is wrapped up completely by the garment, the smooth surface of which enhances the intensity of the face. The glance of the eyes is accentuated by the position of the left hand. Grey-yellowish ground with

traces of paint. Height 22 cm. N. Peru, Mochica culture, between 400 and 600 A. D.
Museum für Völkerkunde, Munich.

187. Upper right: Clay figure of a drummer with his (or her) hour-glass shaped drum under the right arm. From the same tomb as the two other figures on this plate. Height 13 cm. Chicama Valley, N. Peru. Mochica culture, between 400 and 600 A. D.
Museum für Völkerkunde, Munich.
Upper left: Clay figurine without paint, from the same tomb as the two other figures on this plate. Apparently cast in a mould. Height 7.5 cm. Chicama Valley, N. Peru. Mochica culture, between 400 and 600 A. D.
Musum für Völkerkunde, Munich.
Lower left and right: Head and arms of a helmeted warrior on the base of a drum (?). Clay figurine without paint, from the same tomb as the two upper figures of this plate. Height 9.5 cm. Chicama valley, N. Peru. Mochica culture, between 400 and 600 A. D.
Museum für Völkerkunde, Munich.

188. Clay bottle in the shape of a squatting blind man with individually formed features. Blind persons appear often in Mochica sculpture, as do figures or heads of mutilated and sick (see the following plate). As there was no such thing as *genre* subjects in the art of these ancient peoples, we cannot but suppose these figures to have had some significance in religious life. The rendering of the blind in Mochica art was defined as strikingly accurate by Dr. E. Gaffron, experienced opthalmologist and renowned collector of Old Peruvian art. As in many squatting figures of this type, it is only the head that matters and is executed in detail while the rest is treated summarily with the arms and hands modelled superficially and conventionally. (The fist in pl. 190 teaches us that it was no lack of skill that led to this sort of treatment). Head, hands, and handle in Indian red; face-paint in dark stripes; garment and head-dress, cream-white. Height 21 cm. Northern Peru, Mochica culture. Between 400 and 600 A. D.
Museum für Völkerkunde, Munich.

189. Head of a mutilated or sick person, carrying a fox-head (as a symbol or disguise) at his forehead. Front view of a clay bottle. Similar representations are not rare in Mochica art; they are likely to have had some particular meaning (cp. pl. 188

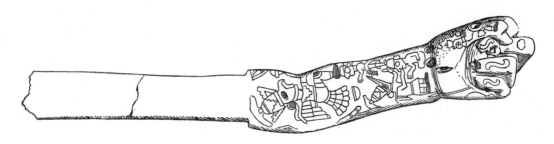

Forearm of carved bone (spatula), with engraved figures and turquoise and pyrites inlay. From the Santa Valley, Northern coast. After: A short guide to American Antiquities, British Museum.

above). If the head of a slain enemy, particularly that of a distinguished warrior or a chief, was represented, the purpose may have been to render serviceable to the victor the strength of the dead. An Old Mexican conception, on the other hand, had it that lepers or syphilitics, suffering from open boils came into the rain-god's domain (according to Sahagun; cp. Krickeberg, *Märchen der Azteken, Inka, Maya und Muiska*, Jena 1928, p. 30). Colours: cream-white and Indian-red; on the face which is in the natural tone of the clay, there are traces of a net-like pattern in black lines. Height of the whole vessel ca. 25 cm. Northern Peru. Mochica culture, between 400 and 600 A. D.

H. and M. Gaffron Collection, Chicago.

190. Forearm of dark greyish-yellow clay. The hand is clenched in a fist with the middle finger projecting: position characteristic of the sling, as used by the god of lightning, lord of thunder and rain in the mountains, according to the ancient myths. There exist several kindred smaller forearms of carved bone, which on the back of the hands bear small S-snakes; the S-curves – likely to be symbols of lightning – run toward the root of the middle finger as though the flashes thence were to be discharged by means of the sling (turquoise inlay; see illustration above; British Museum; cf. Joyce, *American Anthropologist*, N. S. X, 1908, 16–23).

It is reported that a statue of Viracocha, a deity of the mountain folk hot clearly definable as a divine creator or as a traditional heroic figure had one fist raised. And, in a famous ode recorded by Blas Valera and handed down to us by Garcilasso de la Vega (Commentarios Reales, libro II, cap. XXVII), Viracocha appears as the god of thunder

and lightning who smashes his sister's rain-urn so that it rains, snows, or hails. It would be tempting to identify the present fragment as the Fist of Viracocha. However, it is unknown to us whether or not Viracocha, though at one time, worshipped throughout the mountains, was venerated also by the people of the Mochica culture; even so there is little doubt that the meaning of the fragment is basically the same as in the case of Viracocha's fist. Length 33 cm. N. Peru. Mochica culture, between 400 and 600 A. D. Museum für Völkerkunde, Munich.

191. Clay bottle, greyish yellow toned, with mythical scene in relief: An animal-headed deity encircled by snakes seizes the tuft of hair of a woman whose child is sitting in a wrapper. This is a good example of the vigorous relief art of the Mochica culture and appears also on black clay bottles. Chicama Valley, N. Peru. Mochica culture, between 400 and 600 A. D.
Private Collection.

192. Fragment of a head (forming part of a clay vessel). Found as fragment in the anterior shaft of a cave-tomb at Pacatnamú (N. Peruvian coast) in 1938. Forms reminiscent of chased metal (copper or gold) work. Height 10 cm. Early Mochica culture, about 400 A. D.
Museum für Völkerkunde, Munich.

193–197. Clay vessel in the shape of a squatting blind man (cp. pl. 188). View of the vessel and the head alone, taken from various angles. One of the finest sculptural works of Mochica art. The profile (pls. 195, 196) may well be compared with profiles of Renaissance portrait busts (e. g. that of Cosimo Medici). On the garment, traces of creamy white colour; the scarf around the shoulders in Indian red. Height 22 cm. Chicama

44

Valley, N. Peru. Mochica culture, between 400 and 600 A. D. Private Collection.

198–199. Small head, treated somewhat summarily but very effectively. Sketchy paint in white and dark red-brown. Height 12.8 cm. From the same tomb as the following head. Chicama Valley, N. Peru. Mochica culture, between 400 and 600 A. D. Private Collection.

200. Portrait head in clay ('Savonarola'), with traces of a white slip. Height 11 cm. Huaca de la Campana, Pampa de Jaguey. Chicama Valley, N. Peru. Mochica culture, between 400 and 600 A. D. Private Collection.

201. Small portrait head of a one-eyed man. Height 12 cm. N. Peru. Mochica culture, between 400 and 600 A. D.

H. and M. Gaffron Collection, Chicago.

202. Head of a woman (formed on a clay bottle), with traces of creamy white and Indian red paint. Female heads are rare among the Mochica portraits. Height 29.3 cm. Chicama Valley (?), N. Peru. Mochica culture, between 400 and 600 A. D. Formerly in the H. and M. Gaffron Collection; now lost.

203. Portrait head shaped out of a clay bottle (traces of handle and spout still visible). Turban-like head-dress with patterns in dark India red; at the chin, traces of face-paint (tattooing ?). Height 32 cm. Chicama Valley, N. Peru. Mochica culture, between 400 and 600 A. D. Private Collection.

204–205. Portrait head of greyish black clay (profile and front views), with turban-like head-dress and bands. Height 17 cm. (without handle). Chicama Valley, N. Peru. Mochica culture, between 400 and 600 A. D.

Museum für Völkerkunde, Munich.

206. Small portrait head of clay, with dark crimson-red paint. Fragmentary. At one side of the head a rearing snake. Portrait of an unusually ferocious expression. Outstanding example of the Mochica culture. Height 10 cm. Chicama Valley, N. Peru. Mochica culture, between 400 and 600 A. D. Rafael Larco Hoyle Collection, Museo Chiclín, near Trujillo.

207. Portrait head of clay, painted in cream-white and dark India red. The ornaments on the 'turban' are abbreviated renderings of the Raya, the thornback. Profiles resembling the present one, particularly in regard to the nose, I observed occasionally at Cuzco and nearby in 1938 among young Quechua Indians. Height 10 cm. N. Peru., Chicama region. Mochica culture, between 400 and 600 A. D.

Linden-Museum, Stuttgart; Sutorius Collection.

208. Portrait head of clay, with light and dark face-paint (Day and night ? Dusk ? Realm of the dead ?). The large flower projecting from the head-dress resembles the "cuexcochtemalli", an emblem of the Old Mexican death-god, worn at the nape of the neck (cf. Seler, *Ges. Abhandl. II*, 871 f.); it also recalls a 'paper rosette' as worn by the dancers participating in a dead king's obsequies (Seler, ibid., p. 749; Saville, *Manabí, II*, pl. LXXXVI right). On the head-band, at the forefront, the almost ubiquitous ornament or symbol of stepped angular volutes appears. Middle of the face unpainted; to the right and left, dark India red. Height 17.7 cm. (without handle and spout). Chicama region, N. Peru. Mochica culture, between 400 and 600 A. D.

H. and M. Gaffron Collection, Chicago.

209. Portrait head, clay, with streaks left by a modelling tool. Chicama region. N. Peru. Mochica culture, between 400 and 600 A. D.

Museum für Völkerkunde, Munich.

210. Portrait head of clay, showing traces of a whitish slip. Compare the low bridge of the nose with those of the heads in pls. 207 and 213. This head typifies the great variety of types manifest in these portraits which as far as we know all belong to the same cultural environment. The carriers of that culture must have looked as different as the individuals portrayed in pls. 198–225. Height 16 cm. (without handle). Chicama region, N. Peru. Mochica culture, between 400 and 600 A. D.

H. and M. Gaffron Collection, Chicago.

211. Portrait head of a one-eyed man, clay. (The right eye is blind.) Face unpainted; head-band, scarf, and ear-discs cream-white. The face was not cast in a mould, as in most cases, but modelled with a tool, the traces of which are visible everywhere: original sculptured work. Height 39 cm. Chicama region, N. Peru. Mochica culture, between 400 and 600 A. D.

H. and M. Gaffron Collection, Chicago.

212. Portrait head of clay, showing the hieroglyphical image of the thornback, symbol of the sea, in the head-band. Height 19 cm. Chicama region, N.Peru. Mochica culture, between 400 and 600 A.D.

Linden-Museum, Stuttgart, Sutorius Collection.

213. Portrait head of grey clay, showing an uncommonly narrow face with a mouth cut slightly slanting. No doubt the portrait of a distinguished personality. At the temples, on both sides of the head, there are birds that appear to hide their heads under their wings as if asleep. The ear-discs are likely to represent golden settings with large discs of turquoise in the centre. One of the most peculiar types among these renowned portraits, somewhat European in appearance. Found in a rectangular shaft-tomb of the Mochica culture (between 400 and 600 A. D.), near the top of the hill of Facalá, Chicama valley, N. Peru. Height (without handle) 16 cm.
Museum für Völkerkunde, Munich.

214–215. Portrait head of clay, representing an obviously young person ('the cornet') of composed bearing and expression. The face is partly left unpainted, partly painted in dark India red (cp. pl. 208). On the head-bands there appear snakes rushing down over a jagged spiral. Marks of a modelling tool are proof of this head being original work. Height (without handle) 15 cm. Chicama region, N. Peru. Mochica culture, between 400 and 600 A. D.
H. and M. Gaffron Collection, Chicago.

216–217. Portrait head in clay of a man with thick neck. Remarkable for its highly individual treatment. Greyish to yellowish white slip. Height ca. 30 cm. Chicama Valley, N. Peru. Mochica culture, between 400 and 600 A. D.
Private Collection.

218–219. Portrait head of a 'typical' Indian (i. e., of the type of the aboriginal population of North America). The paint again shows a division of the face in light (natural clay tone) and dark (India red) zones, which perhaps are meant to symbolize the fact that the portrayed figure belongs to the nether world. On the head-band, sea-demons (sea-snakes). Height (without handle) 15 cm. Chicama region, N. Peru. Mochica culture, between 400 and 600 A. D.
H. and M. Gaffron Collection, Chicago.

220–221. Large portrait head, the face of which is unpainted. Plain head-band and scarf. One of the most powerfully expressive among this series of portraits, with a mouth so sensitively modelled as to rival that of the fragment from Tiahuanaco in pl. 120. Apparently taken from a mould, a second cast of which is however unknown. Height 21.6 cm. Chicama region, N. Peru.

Mochica culture, between 400 and 600 A. D.
H. and M. Gaffron Collection, Chicago.

222–223. Large portrait head of clay ('the ruler'), ranking among the first-rate achievements of Mochica portrait art. No second cast of this head is known to the writer. Across the forehead, a dark red stripe: from the eyes downward, broad stripes with bordering lines similar to those in the large monolithic head of a god in flat relief from Tiahuanaco (now in La Paz): a strange parallel between these otherwise so different sculptural works. As often in ancient Peruvian art, the meaning appears to be the same in both cases while the forms differ with the various tribes and cultures. There are traces of paint also at the neck. In the head-band appears once more the hieroglyphically abbreviated image of the Raya, the thornback. From its frequent application as a symbolical ornament on the head-bands of portrait heads as well as whole figures, in vase paintings, and even at the outer wall of the Mochica Pyramid (pl. 168), it would appear that the Raya had occupied an important place in the religious conceptions of the Mochica folk. Height (without handle) 28 cm. Chicama region, N. Peru. Mochica culture, between 400 and 600 A. D.
H. and M. Gaffron Collection, Chicago.

224–225. Portrait head of clay. A comparison of this noble work of Mochica art with the heads shown in pls. 210–212, 217–223 will bear out the wide range of individuality within that culture. The nose resembles that in pl. 207. Height 21 cm. Chicama region, N. Peru. Mochica culture, between 400 and 600 A. D.
H. and M. Gaffron Collection, Chicago.

226. Fragment of a tapestry. Light central field in a dark frame, surrounded by other light-coloured panels. In the centre is depicted a gable-roofed house, a temple, full of gods and demons. On the roof there appear mace-heads; the rafters are terminated by snake-heads. Above the house are whirling all sorts of aerial spirits. In the middle of the temple, a powerful figure, unfortunately half destroyed; with his right hand he seems to perform some ritual act. Two feathers with snake-heads are suspended from his girdle. A fox-headed demon to the left holds erect a huge sceptre of state with three cubic rattles, reminiscent of Tiahuanaco style sceptres. Underneath the fox-headed one, two attendants occupy themselves with what appears to be a piece of furniture, while an ex-

cited animal-headed spirit beats the air in front of the temple wall. A bird with vulture-like bill hovers above the hand of the main figure. A very similar scene is known from a Mochica vase painting hailing from the Chicama region (Museum für Völkerkunde, Berlin; cf. Lehmann-Doering, *Kunstgeschichte des alten Peru*, Berlin 1924, fig. 9 left). Star-like eyes are shining forth here and there from the darkness of the framing lines. Two smaller snake-rafter houses can be made out in the fragmentary outer panels; the one in the lower left portion is distinctly recognizable: the gable set with mace-heads; the whirling spirits above the roof; two figures facing each other in the interior. The left figure has an animal-head and a tail; the right one, a human head. Between them, a long sceptre-like staff ending, on top, in a human head; below, in an animal-head. With this unique tapestry we get a glimpse of an almost unknown world of gods, more fully represented than in the vase paintings, and in colours, whereas the vase paintings are only dark brown on a yellowish-white ground. The colours, it is true, are not as bright as those in the textiles of Paracas, Nazca, and of the Tiahuanaco style from the middle and southern Peruvian coast. This cannot only be due to their state of decay. Rather, we have to assume that as seen the vase paintings' bright colours were not favoured by the Mochica artists, and that while creating polychrome designs they gave preference to subdued hues. Yellow, brown, and, occasionally, red appear to have been the chief pigments. A warm sheen as of dim ancient gold is spread over these textiles, and it is this dull golden tone which mainly impresses the onlooker.

The weft is of fine wool, while the warp is of cotton. No patterned textiles that could safely be ascribed to the Mochica culture – which I assign to the period between 400 and 600 A. D. – had become known until the discovery of the image weavings in the shaft-tomb E I of the Pacatnamú site in 1938 (cf. also Lila O'Neale, and A. L. Kroeber, *Textile periods in Ancient Peru:* Univ. Calif. Publicat. Arch. Ethnol. vol. 28, 1930, p. 41). Remnants of Mochica textiles were brought to light during the excavations of Duncan Strong at Viru; I found unquestionable small Mochica fragments among Strong's collections in the American Museum of Natural History in New York. I have not seen the textiles reportedly found during Rafael Larco's excavations. There can be no question that on account of its imagery the tapestry here reproduced remains, even in its fragmentary state, one of the most important textiles of Ancient Peru and Ancient America. Together with a second tapestry found on the chest of the skeleton in the shaft-tomb E I, it forms something like a Codex Aureus of Peru's ancient past.

Diagonal length of the fragment 70 cm. Ruin-city of Pacatnamú (at the mouth of the Rio Yequetepeque, north of Pacasmayo), North Peruvian coast; shaft-tomb E I (a report on the Pacatnamú finds is being prepared and will appear at Verlag Kohlhammer, Stuttgart in 1952).

Museo Nacional de Arqueología, Lima.

227. Fragment of an embroidered weaving from the Mochica culture, about 400 to 600 A. D. Found in 1938 in the rubble left by treasure diggers. The snake-headed rays proceeding from the squarish faces in each of the quadrangles prove that this work has to be considered a Mochica textile. These heads perfectly match those on the rafters of the snake-house in pl. 226; the 'star-eyes' in the dark framing borders around the temple picture in the latter fragment correspond to the cross-designs in the framing squares of the present fragment. Cross-shaped 'star-eyes' distinguish also the heads of the eight rays issuing from the stiffly rendered central faces of a moon-god or star-god. This fragment, too, has a pale golden tone, and only some small details, such as the eyes, show other colours. Length 102 cm. Material: wool and cotton. Pacatnamú, N. Peruvian coast.

Museo Nacional de Arqueología, Lima.

228. Top: Golden flasks, trays, feather-pins and collars (?) of a type ascribed in most cases to the Chimú culture. However, the *décor*, notably that of the tray rims, as well as the shape of the bulbous carinated bottles, rather make one think of early Mochica forms (around 400 A. D.) or even of the earliest great culture in North Peru and possibly the entire West of South America: that of Chavín. The feather-pins come very close to similar broad golden feathers with engraved images of deities in Tiahuanaco style in the Munich Museum für Völkerkunde.

American Museum of Natural History, New York.

Bottom: Pole-top of copper consisting of three figures: Principal figure: An owl-shaped deity with human legs. In front of it kneels a small human figure while a follower of this deity carrying an animal's tail and leaning on a heavy stick stands at his side. Parts of the group are gilded. The figure of the owl-shaped god is inlaid with turquoise (visible to the left of its front and to the right of its back). Height of the group (here somewhat enlarged): 3.5 cm. Total length of the pole: 21.5 cm. Mochica culture, 400 to 600 A. D.

Outstanding example of Early Peruvian miniature metal sculpture.

Norbert Mayrock Collection.

229. Miniature art of the Mochica culture (between 400 and 600 A. D.), made of copper.

Upper left: Vulture-like bird holding in its mouth a head. Dusty green patina. Length: 7 cm.

Norbert Mayrock Collection.

Lower left: Twisted animal, as though skeletonised (embryo? I know of another animal's embryo, rendered in relief, on a vase fragment found near the pass between Faclo and Guadalupe, Jequetepeque Valley, N. Peru. Cp. M. Schmidt, *Kunst und Kultur von Peru*, p. 394, a similar animal is reproduced at the lower left), where Greenish and bluish patina. Length: 5 cm.

Norbert Mayrock Collection.

Right: Chisel or knife-shaped tool, crowned with figure of a warrior carrying club and shield. The form of the mouth shaped like a horizontal 8 is an element common to Mochica as well as Chavín art and characterizes the figure as a superhuman being belonging to the class either of gods or demons (cp. pl. 176). In the cavities of the figure bright, greenish patina. Height 14 cm.

Norbert Mayrock Collection.

230. Large mask of a mummy (?). Gold-copper alloy; eyes of shell. For the rendering of the eye-lids, compare the clay fragment in pl. 192. Perforations at the upper margin of the mask may have served to affix a crown or some head-dress. The ears are attached; the ornamental discs they had held in their wide orifices have disappeared, perhaps because these discs consisted of perishable material (wood with inlay of turquoise?). Turquoise incrusted wooden ear-discs were actually found at Pacatnamú. A green patina covers the surface of the metal. If any kinship can be established, it is in the heads from Pacheco

(pls. 109–113). These do have the same tendency of suppressing individuality and portrait-like detail in favour of monumental grandeur and typification toward the divine. This mask, however, was discovered in a subterranean chamber under the Huaca de la Luna ('Sanctuary of the Moon') near Moche (N. Peru) and it is generally agreed that this sanctuary belongs to the Mochica culture; the mask, therefore, also belongs to Mochica, possibly early Mochica, whereas the Pacheco heads are definitely established examples of the coastal Tiahuanaco style. Both styles, early Mochica and coastal Tiahuanaco, are separated however, according to current opinion, not only regionally, but also chronologically by centuries, the Mochica style being taken as the unquestionably older one. The problem cannot be discussed here, but it seems certain to me that the affinities between the mask from the Huaca de la Luna and the heads from Pacheco point to interconnections, which are further corroborated by the wooden incrusted mummy mask from Pachacamac in pl. 96; in short, there is a network of filiations there, of which at present we know only a few threads. (Cp. my study on *Tonplastik aus Nazca* IPEK, 1927, pp. 67 ff.) Huaca de la Luna near Moche, N. Peruvian coast, Early Mochica culture, about 400 to 500 A. D. Height 26 cm.

Stuttgart, Sutorius Collection.

231. Demon-head of clay, unpainted, with circular eyes (of the dead?) and large fangs as of a beast of prey. Formal treatment reminiscent of woodcarving. Instead of the ear-discs there are here animal-heads suspended on rings. From the forehead, two animal-heads in the round are projecting, the style of which is no more typical of Mochica than the head as a whole. Actually, the work does belong to Mochica, but through its style points farther back in time, that is, to the Chavín style.

Height 13 cm. Chicama Valley, N. Peru. Earliest Mochica culture, about 400 A. D. or earlier.

Private Collection.

232. Mother and child. Clay sculptural group, with traces of paint. From the point of view of style, the group is closely related to the big Moche mask in pl. 230, and hence to the head from Pacheco. Moreover, Pacheco yielded also a Mother-and-child sculpture (pl. 112); the mother's face there resembles that in this group, which formally is

Stone relief on the so-called Tello obelisk, Chavín de Huantar. Copied by Rojas Ponce.
After Tello.

treated more rigidly and severely than the former. This group belongs to those works which, bespeaking far-reaching interrelations, appear to date back to the first centuries A. D. Height 15.5 cm. Chicama Valley, N. Peru. Early Mochica culture, about 400 A. D.

Private collection.

233. Clay bottle with yellowish-white saw-teeth zones around the belly, the outlines of which are incised. The bulging hollow handle, the slightly projecting ring around the spout, and the technique of incising the ornamental outlines are features this early Mochica vessel shares with that part of the older Chavín culture which in the Pacatnamú area gradually waned and was transformed into the Mochica culture. In the Chicama Valley, too, and in tombs excavated by Max Uhle in the vicinity of the pyramids of Moche, this older culture still asserts itself in some of the paintings and reliefs. Height ca. 20 cm. Chicama region, N. Peru. Early Mochica culture, about 400 A. D. or earlier.

H. and M. Gaffron Collection, Chicago.

234. Bottle with conspicuously flat body of dark grey clay. On the upper face, the image of a god in relief with a beast of prey face, snake-crown and snake-belt with its end swinging sideways. On the lower part, around the foot-rim, a frieze of interlocked hooks and steps. (cp. the Chongoyape relief, N. Peru). The passionate art of Chavín, also its representations of terrible gods, is still fully

alive in this object which to our present knowledge seems entirely foreign to Mochica. Decidedly we have to deal here with the Chavín art. To all appearances, this art here, at Pacatnamú, was coeval with the early Mochica art: the bottle was found in the same tomb as the tapestry shown in pl. 226, which undoubtedly is a Mochica product, if indeed our present conception of what Mochica culture was, is correct at all; and a woman buried in the same tomb had her forearms and hands tattooed with figures of purest Mochica style. Surely the late Chavín culture and the beginning of Mochica culture at Pacatnamú in the Yequetepeque Valley were synchronous. This fact is of extraordinary importance because in the Virú Valley farther south, the Chavín cultural stratum has proved stratigraphically separated, according to Duncan Strong's investigations, from that of the Mochica culture by thick layers of two other cultures, 'Salinár' and 'Gallinazo'. There must be sites to the north of the Chicama Valley, undiscovered as yet, where Chavín-Costeño and Mochica will be found to be associated, and where perhaps a style covering both, Chavín *and* Mochica, will come to light. Height 18 cm. Pacatnamú at the mouth of Rio Yequetepeque, North Peruvian coast. Declining Chavín culture: here about 400 A. D. or earlier.

Museo Nacional de Arqueología, Lima.

235. Bottle of black, smooth, light clay shaped as an imaginary head of a deity with features partly

human and partly animal. Only superior craftsmanship at the height of an expressive, flourishing culture could have produced such a work. The iconographic details, eyes with 'eccentric iris' (Kroeber); the two furrowed lobes above the nose; the characteristic teeth and fangs; the peculiarly stylized ears; the roughened vertex with the parallel smooth lines on it; the stout handle and the trimming of the mouth on top; the blackish clay – all point alike to the vessel's belonging to Chavín art in its heyday. However, according to the former owner's communication, the piece was dug up near Ica in southern Peru! This is not unlikely, as there are certain types of vessels of the Paracas-Cavernas culture (cp. pl. 160) to demonstrate that the Chavín culture or one closely related to it, actually had reached those southern valleys. Presumably there do exist further sites, either in the Ica valley or the Nazca Valleys, where ceramics of pure Chavín Costeño style, such as this one, will be found one day.

Height 21 cm. Chavín-Costeño culture, before 400 A. D. Museum für Völkerkunde, Munich.

236. Top: Stone relief on a cornice stone block, at the South Western corner of the 'Castillo' in the ruins of Chavín de Huantar (Eastern slopes of Cordillera Blanca): Demonised Jaguar encircled by snakes. Its strange, scaled tail emanates from a beast of prey's mouth turned into the back of the Jaguar (visible at the left). The tail itself ends in a beast of prey's (or a snake's) head from whose mouth issue the last two segments of the tail. This relief, belonging to the most outstanding works of Chavín art, very clearly shows its preference for swinging curves. Chavín culture, between 200 and 400 A. D.

Bottom: Sacrificial vessel shaped as a Jaguar, with numerous symbolic sculptures; among these an S-shaped snake lying on the Jaguar's flank exactly like the S-shaped snake (with eyes) on the flank of the Jaguar-relief mentioned above. Chavín culture, between 200 and 400 A. D.

University Museum, Philadelphia, Pa., USA.

237. Upper left: Cerro Blanco Temple in the Nepeña Valley, N. Peruvian coast. Colours: brick-red and greenish yellow. Excavations of Julio C. Tello, Chavín culture at the coast, before 400 A. D.

Upper right: Remains of a large clay-modelled and painted figure at Moxeke, Casma Valley, N. Peruvian coast. Excavation of Tello, who is standing below the figure. Colours: White, yellow, black, and red. Coastal Chavín culture before 400 A. D.

Lower right: Jaguar figure in painted clay. Height c. 1.50 m. Punkurí, Nepeña Valley, N. Peruvian coast. Excavation of J. C. Tello. Coastal Chavín culture, before 400 A. D.

Lower left: Monolithic slabs with carved designs. Cerro Sechín Temple, Casma Valley, N. Peruvian coast. Defined as Chavín style. Excavations by J. C. Tello.

238. Two carved stone slabs from the front of the temple of Cerro Sechín, showing trophy heads. Excavations by J. C. Tello. Defined as Chavín style. A primitive if expressive art that calls to mind relief-figures from the Monte Alban, Mexico. Undoubtedly very early, (early first millenium A. D.).

239. Two views of a large clay pot of the Paracas Cavernas culture, found in the Ica Valley, S. Peru, probably in the vicinity of Ocucaje. Two pairs of figures placed crosswise: demons with their heads strangely dissolved into snakes, overtopped by a little figure, and framed by somewhat shapelessly curved snake-like creatures with human heads; a second pair of demons in narrow fields shows the round faces with a kind of serrated nimbus; the figures hold staffs or clubs, and across their bodies run diagonal white bands that cross in the middle – distinct from the crosses worn by the snake-demons. One of the most curious vase paintings from Peru, the primitiveness of which, possibly intentional, contrasts strikingly with the definite knowledge of the religious ideas in these figures. Here, too, an almost hieroglyphical symbolism appears. The outlines of the several fields are incised, and the lacquer-like colour paste was added after firing of the vessel. Colours: yellow, red, bluish green (in the incised contours traces of white).

The specimen undoubtedly belongs (as the specimens on pls. 160 and 162) to the Paracas Cavernas culture, typifying perfectly its singular *cloisonné* pottery. In regard to the figures represented, on the other hand, the vessel seems completely isolated so far, and thus is a new example of the lack of iconographically defined types in the imagery of Paracas Cavernas pointed out by Kroeber (A. L. Kroeber, *Peruvian Archaeology in 1942*, Viking Fund, New York 1944, p. 34). The motives are hardly ever repeated. The

50

feature apt to make the Paracas Cavernas pottery appear as a unity at all is the *cloisonné* technique with incised contours. It is tempting to think of this technique as the common means by which were expressed elements derived from different cultural centres, elements that mixed or blended but did not melt into each other. Height 32 cm. Between ± 0 and 500 A. D. Private Collection.

240. Piece of tapestry showing a white face on black ground. Border in subdued colours. Width: 35 cm. Stylistically difficult to place. Technical characteristics of the fragment as well as formal properties of the head with its piercing eyes rather suggest one of the early Highland cultures as the likely provenance.
Museum für Völkerkunde, Munich; Heinrich Hardt Collection.

BIBLIOGRAPHY

This bibliography includes, besides books intended for the general reader, special studies, particularly those pertaining to chronology and stratigraphy. This may help the reader who wishes to make a more detailed study of the art of Old Peru. Likewise, two of the latest papers on the radiocarbon-method have been mentioned at the end as well as another one on dendro-chronology. Those papers fully cited in the text are not included in this bibliography.

Antze, Gustav, Metallarbeiten aus dem nördlichen Peru: Mitteilungen aus dem Museum für Völkerkunde in Hamburg, XV, Hamburg, 1930.

Baessler, Arthur, Altperuanische Kunst. 4 vols. (Folio) Berlin 1902–1903.

Baessler, Arthur, Altperuanische Metallgeräte. 3 vols. (Folio) Berlin 1906.

Bennett, Wendell C., The Archaeology of the Central Andes: Handbook of South American Indians, vol. 2, The Andean Civilizations. Washington, 1946, pp. 61–147.

Bennett, Wendell C., The Peruvian Co-Tradition: A Reappraisal of Peruvian Archaeology: American Antiquity, vol. XIII, No. 4, Part 2, April 1948, p. 1 ff.

Bennett, Wendell C., and *Junius Bird,* Andean Culture History: American Museum of Natural History, Handbook Series No. 15, New York 1949.

Bingham, Hiram, In the Wonderland of Peru: National Geographic Magazine, vol. 24, No. 4, pp. 387–573. Washington 1913.

Bingham, Hiram, Machu Picchu, a Citadel of the Incas. New Haven 1930.

Bird, Junius, Pre-ceramic Cultures in Chicama and Virú: A Reappraisal of Peruvian Archaeology: American Antiquity, vol. XIII, No. 4, Part 2, April 1948, p. 21 ff.

Carrión Cachot, Rebeca, Julio C. Tello y la Arqueología Peruana. Lima 1948.

Disselhoff, Hans Dietrich, Zur Frage eines Mittel-chimú-Stiles: Zeitschrift für Ethnologie, 71. Jahrg., pp. 129–138.

Disselhoff, Hans Dietrich, Sogenannte "Chavín"-Gefäße im Berliner Museum für Völkerkunde: Baessler-Archiv, vol. XXIII, Berlin 1940, pp. 19–25.

Doering, Heinrich U.-, Altperuanische Kunst·Berlin 1936.

Doering, Heinrich U.-, Auf den Königsstraßen der Inka. Reisen und Forschungen in Peru. Berlin 1941.

Doering, Heinrich U.-, Ceramic Comparisons of Two North Coast Peruvian Valleys: Selected Papers of the XXIXth International Congress of Americanists, New York 1949, Chicago 1951, p. 224 ff.

Fejos, Paul, Archaeological Explorations in the Cordillera Vilcabamba, South Eastern Peru: Viking Fund Publications in Anthropology, No. 3, New York 1944.

D'Harcourt: Raoul, Les textiles anciens du Pérou. Paris 1934.

Kidder II, Alfred, The Position of Pucara in Titicaca Basin Archaeology: A Reappraisal of Peruvian Archaeology: American Antiquity, vol XIII, No. 4, Part 2, April 1948, p. 87 ff.

Krickeberg, Walter, Felsplastik und Felsbilder bei den Naturvölkern Altamerikas. Vol. I. Berlin 1949.

Kroeber, A. L., and *William Duncan Strong,* The Uhle Pottery Collection from Ica: University of California Publications in American Archaeology and Ethnology, vol. 21, No. 3, pp. 95–133, Berkeley 1924.

Kroeber, A. L., The Uhle Pottery from Moche: University of California Publications in American Archaeology and Ethnology, vol. 21, No. 6, pp. 235–264. Berkeley 1925.

Kroeber, A. L., Peruvian Archaeology in 1942: Viking Fund Publications in Anthropology, No. 4, New York 1944.

Kroeber, A. L., Summary and Interpretations: A Reappraisal of Peruvian Archaeology: American Antiquity, vol. XIII, No. 4, Part 2, April 1948, p. 113 ff.

Kroeber, A. L., Art.: Handbook of South American Indians, vol. 5, pp. 411–492. Washington 1949.

Kroeber, A. L., Great Art Styles of Ancient South America: Selected Papers of the XXIXth International Congress of Americanists, p. 207 ff. Chicago 1951.

Kutscher, Gerd, Chimú, eine altindianische Hochkultur, Berlin 1950.

Kubler, George, Towards Absolute Time: Guano Archaeology: A Reappraisal of Peruvian Archaeology: American Antiquity, vol. XIII, No. 4, Part 2, April 1948, p. 29 ff.

Larco Hoyle, Rafael, Los Mochicas, Tomo II (the only volume available to me). Lima 1939.

Larco Hoyle, Rafael, A Culture Sequence for the North Coast of Peru: Handbook of South American Indians, vol. 2, The Andean Civilizations, pp. 149 ff. Washington 1946.

Lehmann: Walter, und Heinrich Doering, Kunstgeschichte des Alten Peru. Berlin 1924.

Levillier, Jean, Paracas, a Contribution to the Study of Pre-Incaic Textiles in Ancient Peru. Paris 1928.

Means, Philip Ainsworth, Ancient Civilizations of the Andes. New York, London 1931.

Means, Philip Ainsworth, A Study of Peruvian Textiles in The Museum of Fine Arts, Boston. Boston 1932.

Middendorf, E. W., Peru. 3 vols. Berlin 1893 to 1895.

Muelle, Jorge C., Necesidades de la Arqueología Peruana: Selected Papers of the XXIXth International Congress of Americanists, 1949, pp. 201 ff. Chicago 1951.

Posnansky, Arthur, Eine prähistorische Metropole in Südamerika. Berlin 1914.

Reiss, Wilhelm, und Stübel, Alphons, Das Totenfeld von Ancon. Folio. Berlin 1880–1887.

Rowe, Jon Howland, An Introduction to the Archaeology of Cuzco: Papers of the Peabody Museum of American Archaeology and Ethnology, Harvard University, vol. XXVII, No. 2. Cambridge 1944.

Rowe, John Howland, On Basic Highland Culture: A Reappraisal of Peruvian Archaeology: American Antiquity, vol. XIII. No. 4, Part 2, April 1948, p. 20 ff.

Schaedel, Richard, Major Ceremonial and Population Centers in Northern Peru: Selected Papers of the XXIXth International Congress of Americanists, 1949, pp. 232 ff. Chicago 1951. (Unfortunately this important paper has only come into my hands during the printing of this book. Otherwise I would have referred to Schaedel's discussion on cult and lay centers on p. 10 of my introduction.)

Schmidt, Max, Über altperuanische Gewebe mit szenenhaften Darstellungen: Baessler-Archiv I, Leipzig und Berlin 1911, pp. 1–61.

Schmidt, Max, Kunst u. Kultur von Peru. Berlin 1929.

Steward, Julian H., A Functional-Developmental Classification of American High Cultures: A Reappraisal of Peruvian Archaeology: American Antiquity, vol. XIII, No. 4, Part 2, April 1948, p. 103 ff.

Strong, William Duncan, Cross Sections of New World Prehistory: Smithsonian Miscellaneous Collections, vol. 104, No. 2. Washington 1943.

Strong, William Duncan, Finding the Tomb of a Warrior God: The National Geographic Magazine, vol. XVI, April 1947, pp. 453–482.

Strong, William Duncan, Cultural Epochs and Refuse Stratigraphy in Peruvian Archaeology: A Reappraisal of Peruvian Archaeology, vol. XIII, No. 4, Part 2, April 1948, p. 93 ff.

Strong, William Duncan, Cultural Resemblances in Nuclear America Parallelism or Diffusion?: Selected Papers of the XXIXth International Congress of Americanists, p. 271 ff. Chicago 1951.

Stübel, Alphons, und Uhle, Max, Die Ruinenstätte von Tiahuanaco. Folio. Leipzig 1892.

Tello, Julio C., Andean Civilization: Proceedings of the Twenty-Third International Congress of Americanists, September 1928, pp. 259–290.

Tello, Julio C., Discovery of the Chavín Culture in Peru: American Antiquity, vol. IX, No. 1, pp. 135–160.

Tello, Julio C., Orígen y desarrollo de las Civilizaciones Prehistóricas Andinas. Lima 1942.

Uhle, Max, Pachacamac, Report of the William Pepper Peruvian Expedition of 1896. Philadelphia 1903.

Uhle, Max, Die Ruinen von Moche: Journal de la Société des Américanistes, vol. 10, pp. 95–117. Paris 1913.

Uhle Max, Zur Chronologie der alten Kulturen von Ica: Journal de la Société des Américanistes, vol. 10, pp. 341–367. Paris 1913.

Valcárcel, Luis E., Cuzco-Archaeology: Handbook of South American Indians, vol. 2, The Andean Civilizations, p. 177 ff. Washington 1946.

Valcárcel, Luis E., Sajsawaman redescubierto: Revista del Museo Nacional, vol. 3, Nos. 1–4, Lima 1934/1935.

Willey, Gordon R., Functional Analysis of Horizon Styles in Peruvian Archaeology: A Reappraisal of Peruvian Archaeology, vol. XIII, No. 4, Part 2, April 1948, p. 8 ff.

On Radiocarbon Methods:

Linné, Sigvald, Radiocarbon Dates: Ethnos, 1950, 3–4. The Ethnographical Museum of Sweden, Stockholm.

Johnson, Frederick, Radiocarbon Dating: American Antiquity, vol. XVII, No. 1, Part 2, July 1951. In the same volume p. 37 ff: *Bird, Junius*, South American Radiocarbon Dates.

On Dendro-Chronology:

Stallings: W. S., Dating Prehistoric Ruins by Tree-Rings: General Series, Bulletin No. 8, Laboratory of Anthropology, 1939; revised edition, 1949. Santa Fé, New Mexico.

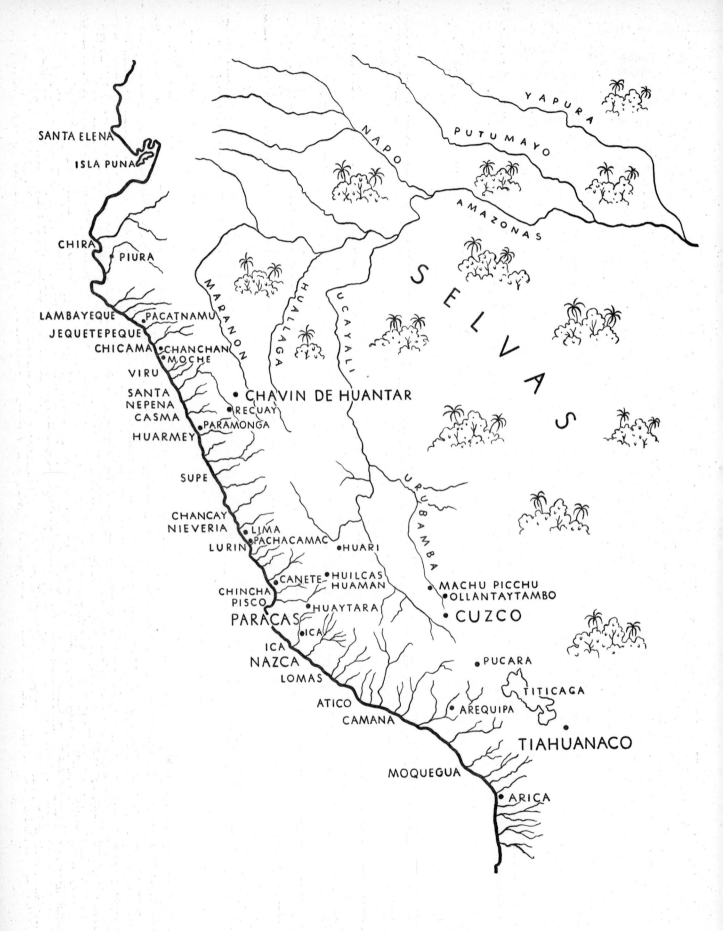

SANTA ELENA

ISLA PUNA

CHIRA

PIURA

LAMBAYEQUE

JEQUETEPEQUE

CHICAMA

VIRU

SANTA

NEPENA

CASMA

HUARMEY

SUPE

CHANCAY

NIEVERIA

LURIN

CHINCHA

PISCO

PARACAS

ICA

NAZCA

LOMAS

ATICO

CAMANA

MOQUEGUA

PACATNAMU

CHANCHAN

MOCHE

RECUAY

PARAMONGA

CHAVIN DE HUANTAR

MARANON

HUALLAGA

UCAYALI

NAPO

PUTUMAYO

YAPURA

AMAZONAS

S E L V A S

URUBAMBA

LIMA

PACHACAMAC

HUARI

CANETE

HUILCAS

HUAMAN

HUAYTARA

ICA

MACHU PICCHU

OLLANTAYTAMBO

CUZCO

PUCARA

TITICAGA

AREQUIPA

TIAHUANACO

ARICA

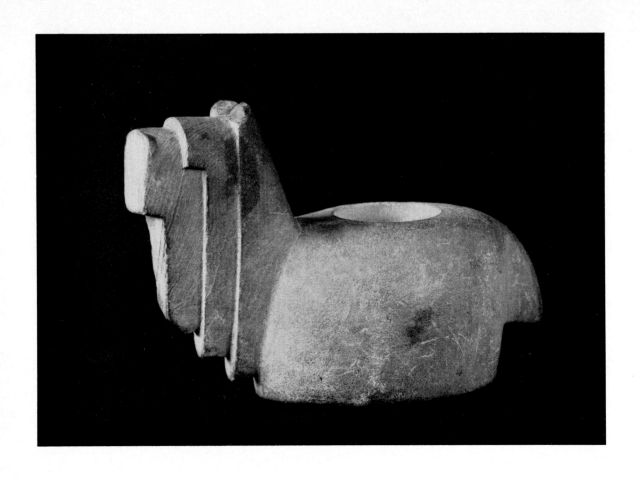

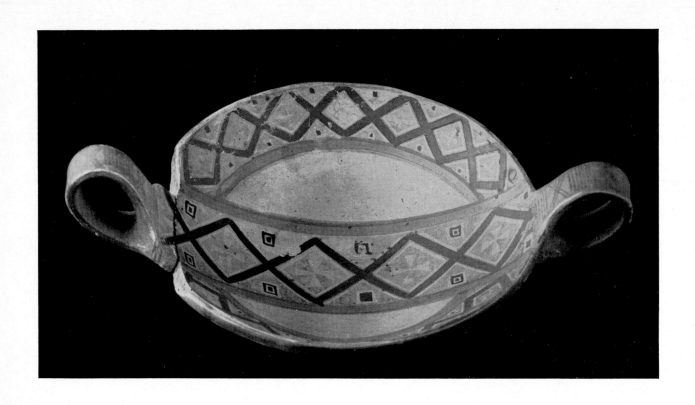

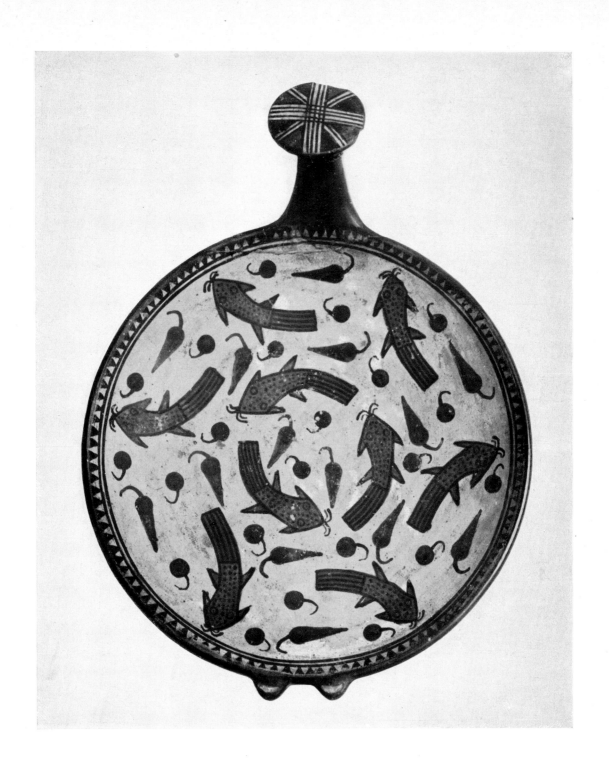

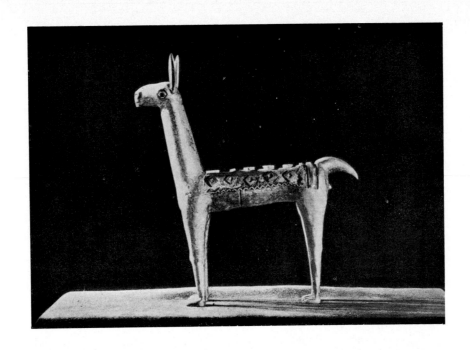

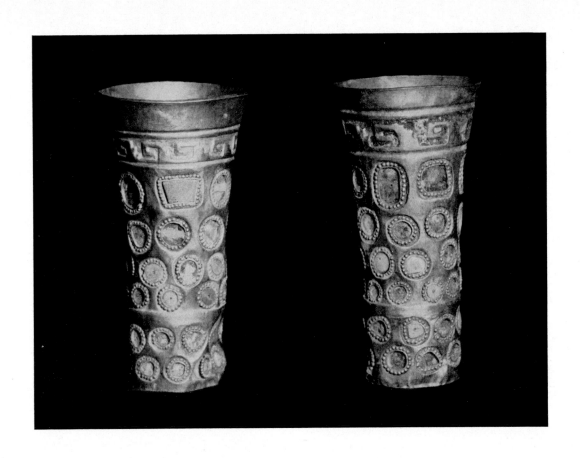

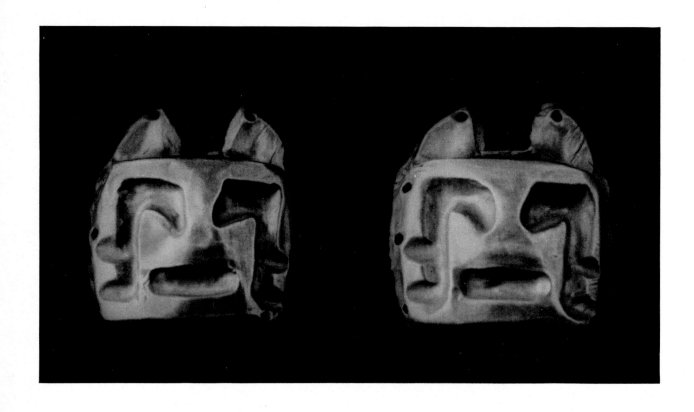

68

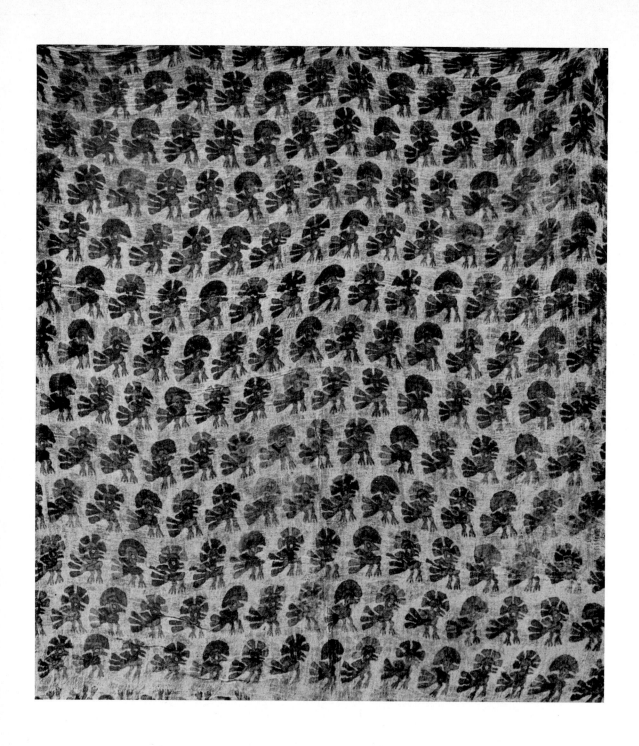

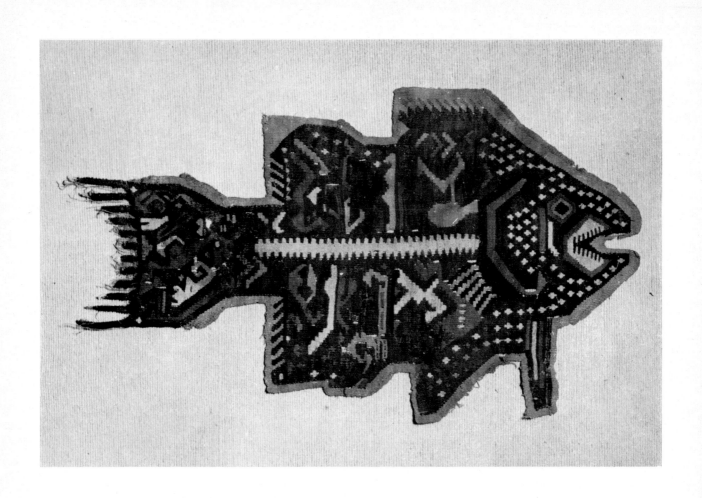

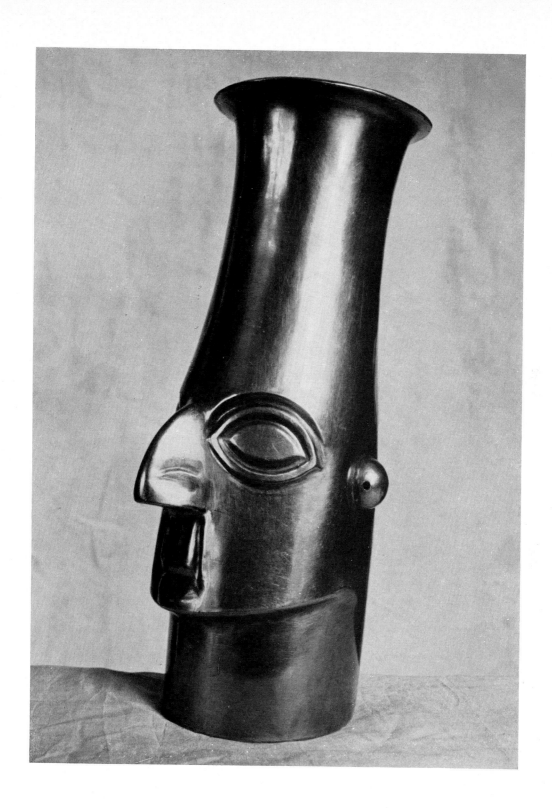

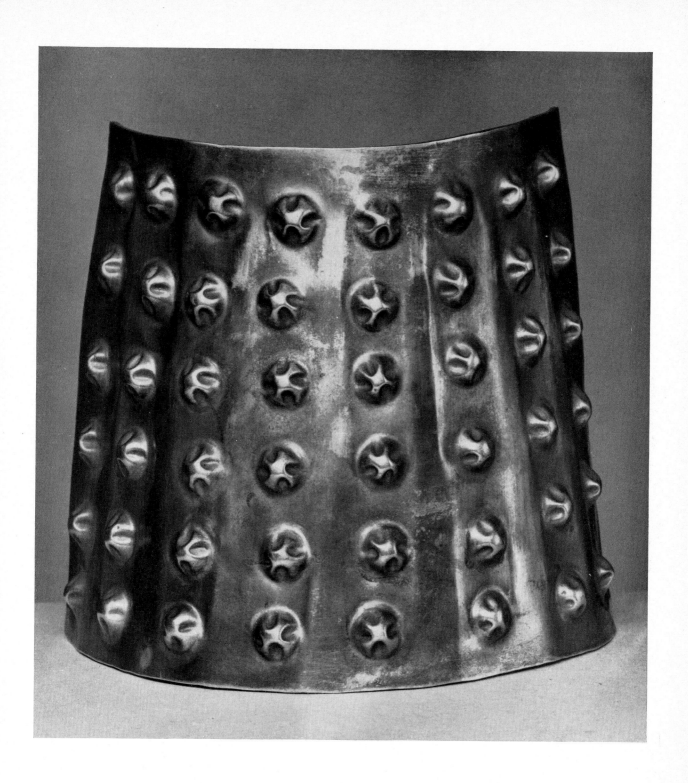

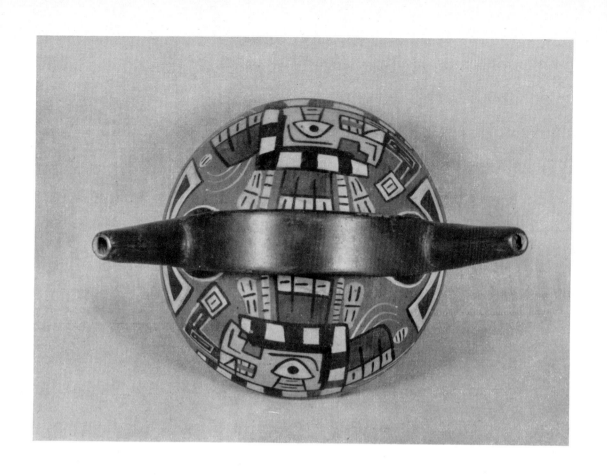

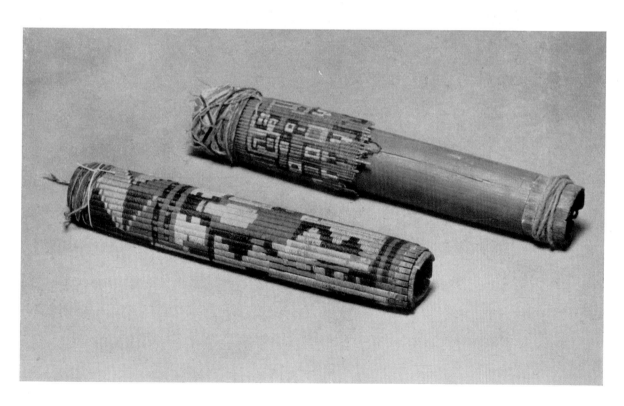

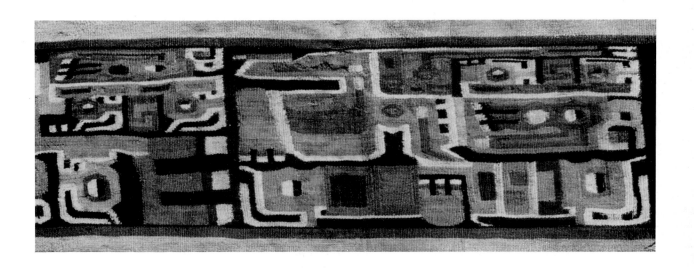

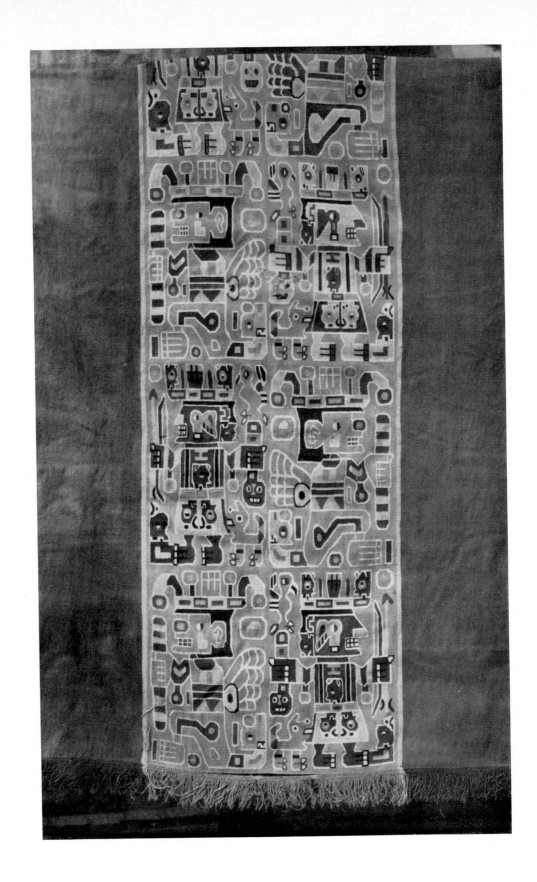

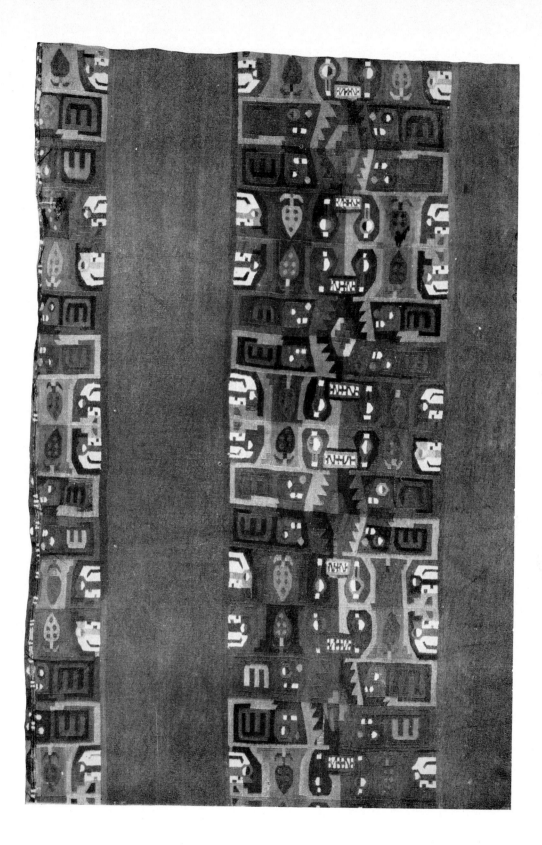

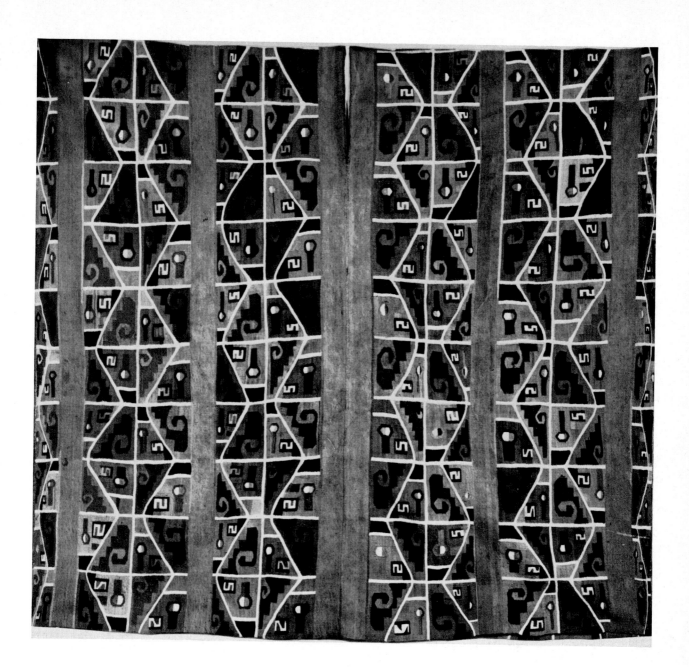

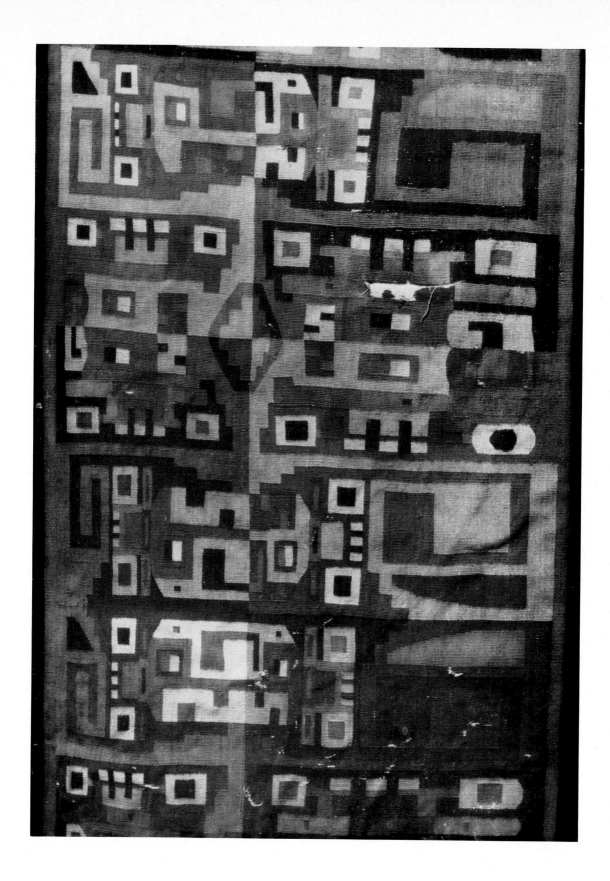

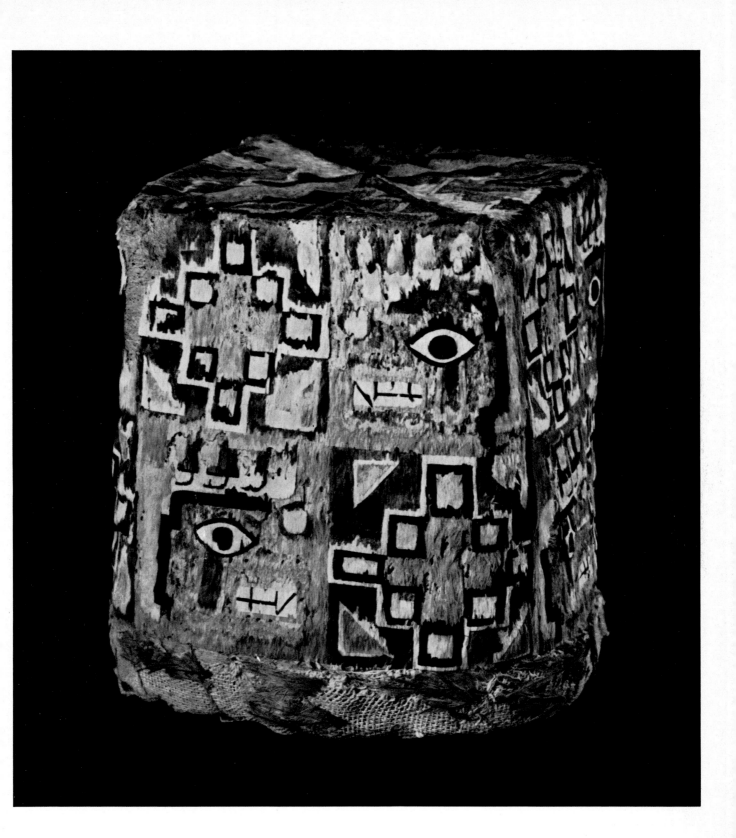

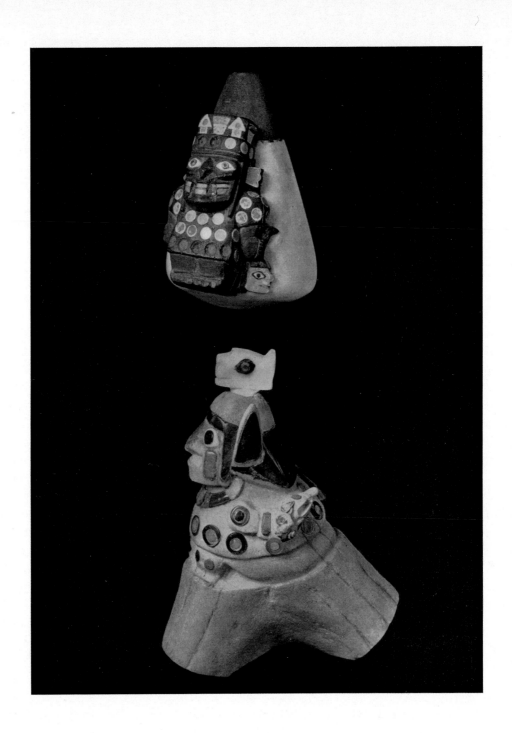

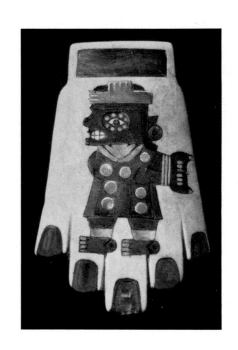

118

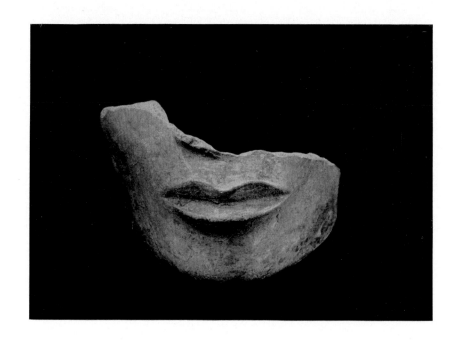

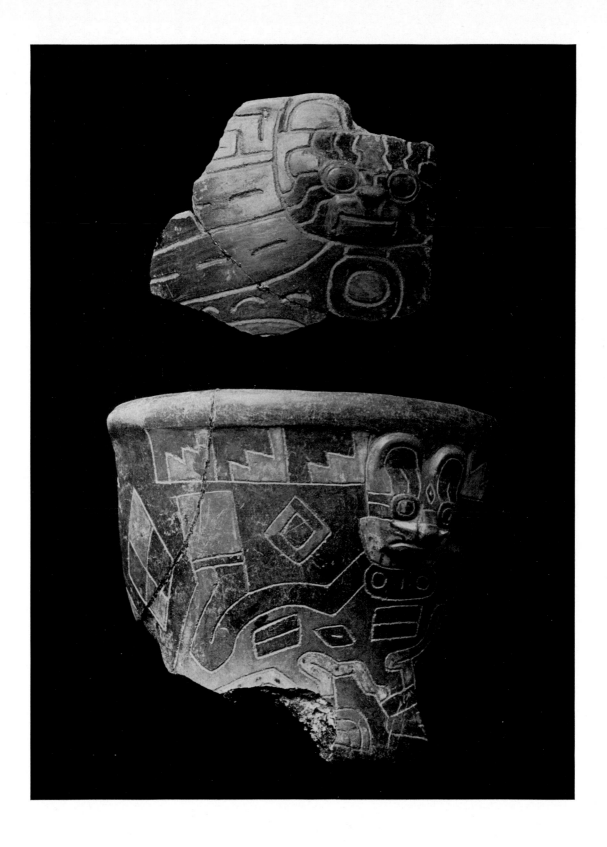

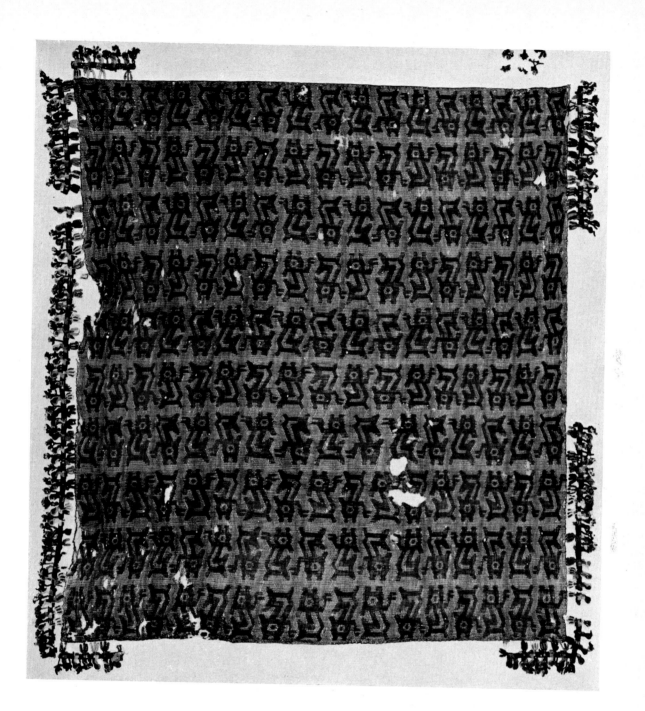

144

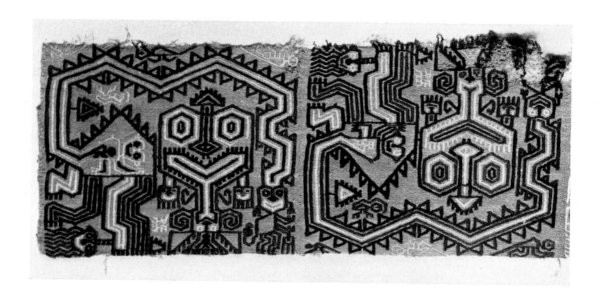

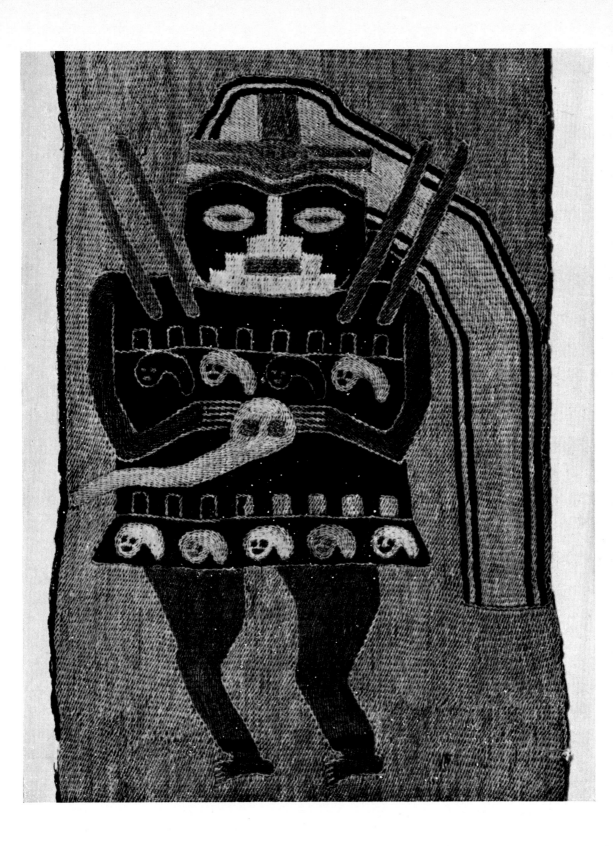

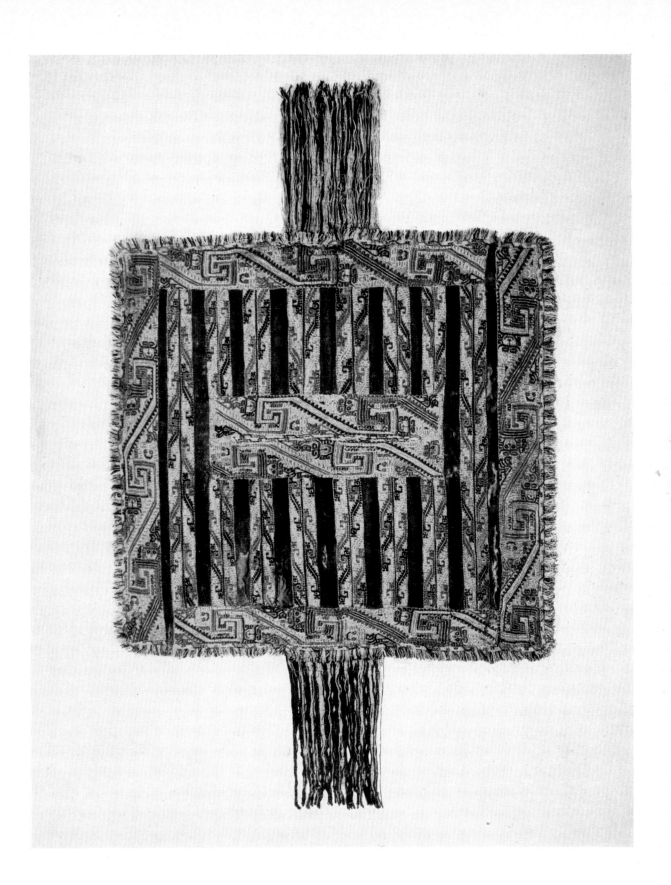

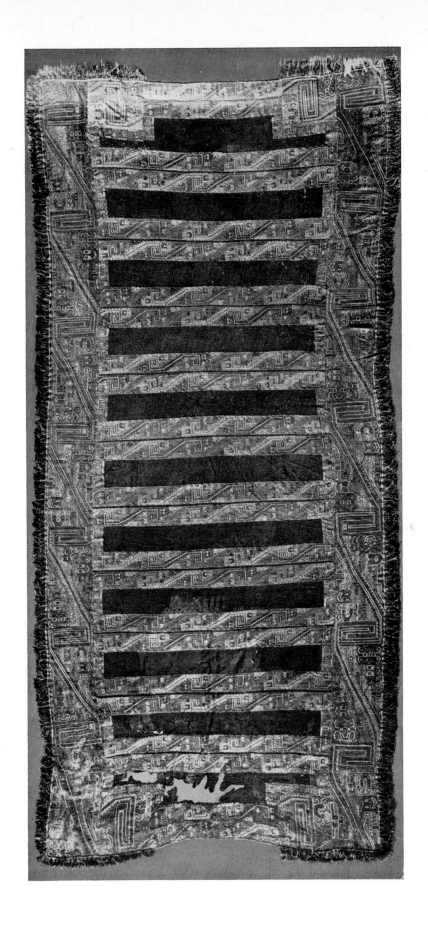

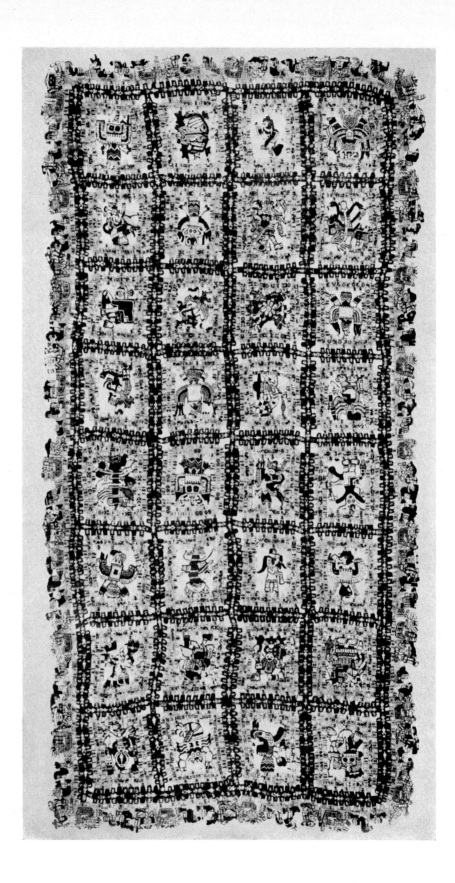

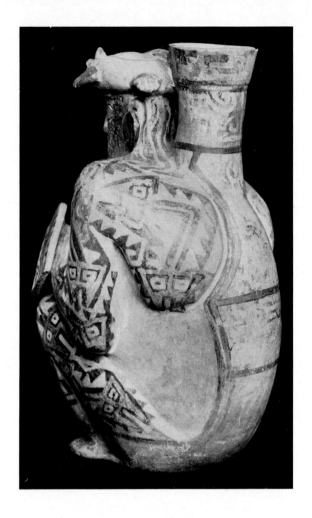

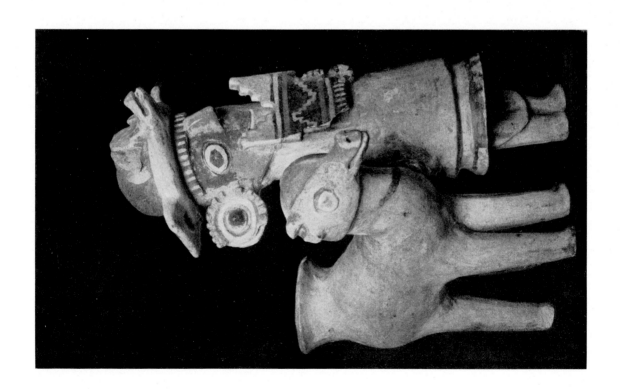

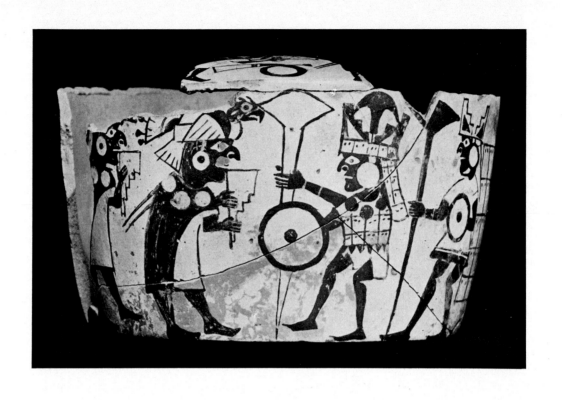

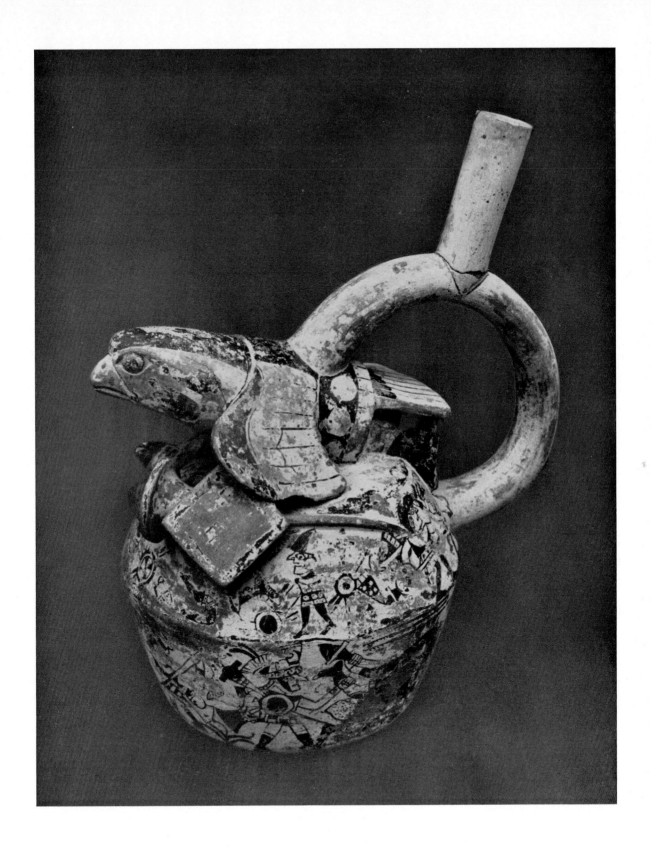

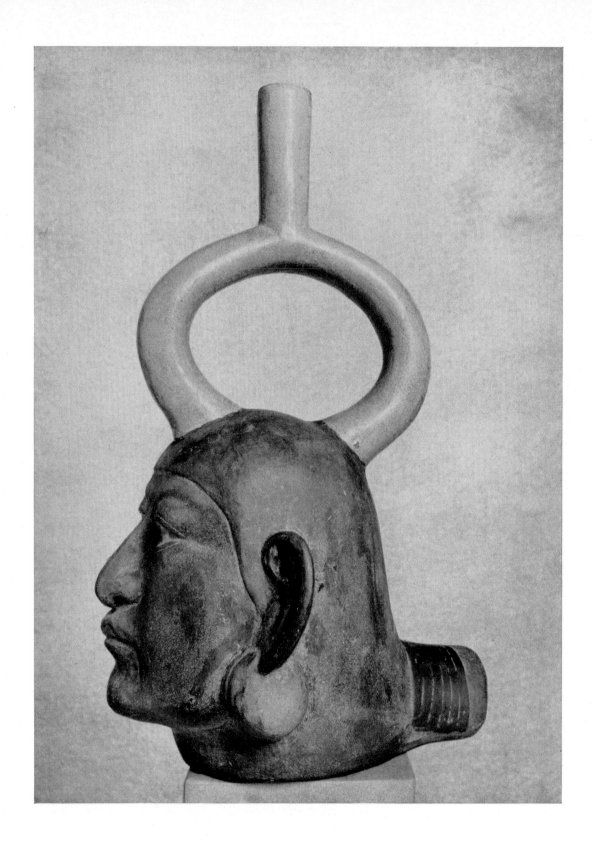

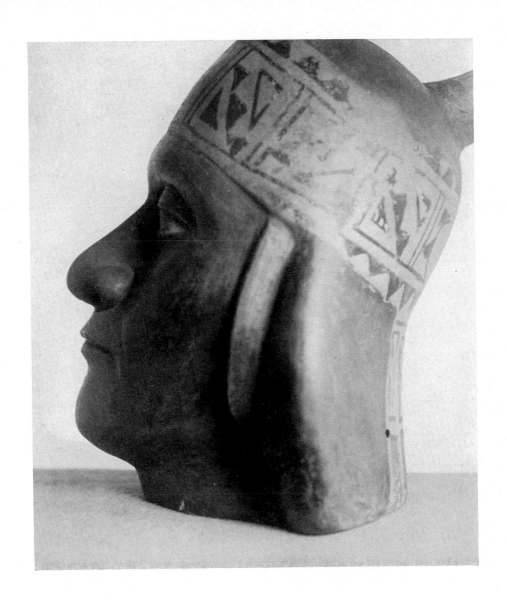

216